Knowledge in a Nutshell™
on Popular Products
Heinz Edition

Charles Reichblum
with John Dryer

D0204209

arpr, inc.

Paperbacks

Knowledge in a Nutshell™ on Popular Products, Heinz Edition is the third book in the *Knowledge in a Nutshell™ series.* The other books are *Knowledge in a Nutshell™ and Knowledge in a Nutshell on Sports™*

KNOWLEDGE IN A NUTSHELL™ ON POPULAR PRODUCTS HEINZ EDITION

ISBN: 0-9660991-1-7

Printed in the United States of America by Geyer Printing Co. Pittsburgh, PA

arpr, inc. Paperbacks edition/May 2000
10 9 8 7 6 5 4 3 2 1

Dedication

To gather all the information for the facts and stories in this book, we consulted many outside reference books and interviewed past and present employees of the H.J. Heinz Company.

We are particularly grateful to Debbie Foster, Director of Corporate Communications at Heinz. Debbie showed incredible patience and good humor with our many questions, and she supplied us with facts we needed.

Special thanks also go to Deb Crosby, General Manager of Quality Assurance and Technical Development at Heinz; Ed Lehew, retired Heinz advertising executive; Liz Watkins, Adjunct Professor at Carnegie Mellon University; Ted Smyth, Senior Vice President, Corporate and Government Affairs at Heinz; Jack Kennedy, General Manager, Strategic Communications at Heinz; authors Eleanor Foa Dienstag, Robert C. Alberts and E.D. McCafferty; Jack Horner and Kristin Sofran of Jack Horner Communications; and Barbara Rodi, our indispensable Administrative Assistant.

Thanks go, too, to Jim Trusilo for the cover illustration and Rob Handley and Tara Taylor of Droz and Associates for the cover design as well as to the many other people who supplied us with information, memories and recipes.

TABLE OF CONTENTS

Preface

There are fascinating stories about products we use every day—how they got their names, who were the people behind them, and the "inside" information on their rise to popularity.

Take ketchup, for instance. How in the world did it get that name, and why is it sometimes spelled "catsup"?

The first two *Knowledge in a Nutshell* books explored the interesting facts and stories about U.S. Presidents, movies, money, geography, health, sports, music and other general topics. This book is the beginning of our series on "Popular Products."

The first *Knowledge in a Nutshell on Popular Products—Heinz Edition* looks inside one of the world's most famous companies and tells the amazing story of its founder along with fun facts about Charlie the Tuna, Morris the 9-Lives Cat, what Britons do with baked beans, how vinegar can help you with household chores, and things you probably never knew about pickles and other products.

We think you'll enjoy reading this book—and then have more fun on your next trip to the supermarket or a restaurant.

ONE

In the Beginning…
From Bankruptcy to Billions

One

In the Beginning...

Why "57" for Heinz?

Surprisingly, although Heinz's "57 Varieties" is one of the most famous slogans in the history of business, the number 57 was NOT—and is NOT—the number of products Heinz sells.

The story begins when the company's owner, Henry Heinz, was riding an elevated train in New York City in 1896. He looked up and saw a car-card advertising 21 styles of shoes. He quickly decided to use that type of slogan for his company.

At the time, Heinz was manufacturing more than 60 products—but Henry thought 57 was a magic, lucky number. According to his diary, the number 57 kept turning in his mind, and so he came up with "57 Varieties." He was so taken with that number, he quickly got off the train and began the work of laying out his advertising plans using 57.

Within a week, "57 Varieties" was appearing in newspapers, on billboards, signboards, and "everywhere else I could find a place to stick it," according to Heinz's diary.

Today, Heinz produces more than 5,700 products, but the company still uses "57."

Who was H. J. Heinz?

The founder of the H.J. Heinz company was Henry John Heinz, born in Pittsburgh, Pennsylvania, in 1844.

His parents, John and Anna, had recently come to America from Germany, and they hoped their son would become a Lutheran minister.

But Henry had other ideas. By the time he was 12, his mother had planted a large vegetable garden behind their home. And that garden would change the career plans for Henry—as well as the eating habits of people all over the world.

Billion-dollar business
started by 12-year-old boy

Henry Heinz, at age 12, began selling produce from his mother's garden to neighbors door-to-door. Four years later, Henry was selling food directly to grocery stores.

At age 19, he was thrilled to make a profit of $25 from selling fresh vegetables. Little did anyone know then that Henry Heinz had started an enterprise which would grow into a worldwide, billion-dollar company.

Today's H.J. Heinz Co. started as Heinz & Noble

By the time he was 25, Henry Heinz was ready to change from being an individual selling his mother's food to forming an actual company to process and market food products.

Henry found a partner, L.C. Noble, and, in 1869, they created the Heinz & Noble Co.

Their business was good for six years—but prosperity would not last.

The Financial Panic of 1875 wiped out Heinz & Noble and sent Henry into bankruptcy. Banks failed. Heinz & Noble had over-bought supplies and found they couldn't pay for them, and couldn't get credit.

Incredibly, Heinz couldn't buy groceries for his own family

It's hard to believe, but Henry Heinz, whose company now supplies food for stores and people all over the world, could NOT buy enough groceries for his own family when he was in bankruptcy.

Today, Heinz food is on millions of tables. Then, he couldn't get enough food for his own. Unbelievable, but true.

In the winter of 1875, the 31-year-old Henry had no cash, and stores that had gladly bought his quality products before his bankruptcy refused to give him credit.

According to his diary, Henry and his wife, Sallie, "suffered tremendous grief. I wish no one such trials," he wrote.

That could have been the end of a great success story for Henry. But, in reality, it was only the beginning.

How Heinz recovered

In his darkest days of bankruptcy, Henry Heinz vowed to pay off all creditors and start again, still believing he had the knack for providing quality food to the public.

Two months after bankruptcy, Henry formed a new company. His brother, John, and a cousin, Frederick, advanced $1,600. His wife had $400 from an inheritance, and Henry borrowed $1,000 from a neighbor.

With total capital of the princely sum of $3,000, Henry launched the F. and J. Heinz Co., using the initials of his brother and cousin who had contributed money.

Henry didn't have much capital, but he did know food; he also knew how to promote it, and he became a true marketing genius.

In the Beginning…

Surprisingly, Heinz's first product was NOT ketchup

Although ketchup is the most famous Heinz product today, and is called the "flagship" product by the company, it wasn't the first made.

When Henry Heinz started the company in 1869, his first product was bottled horseradish, with his mother's recipe.

The reason Henry chose horseradish was because it was a popular condiment among the large German and English immigrant populations in the Pittsburgh neighborhood where he lived.

Ketchup didn't come next, either

After introducing bottled horseradish to get the Heinz company started, Henry Heinz turned next to celery sauce, mustard, sauerkraut, and three kinds of pickles.

Ketchup didn't come along until seven years after the company was founded.

Heinz's bottled ketchup made its way into stores for the first time in 1876. But as late as the

1880s, the top-selling Heinz product was pickles.

Ketchup eventually overtook pickles as the company's No. 1 seller and has remained there ever since.

The clear glass bottle clears the way

Until the late 1800s, most homemakers spent long hours making their own condiments, such as ketchup and horseradish.

They were reluctant to buy new ready-made commercial ketchups and horseradish because some manufacturers used cheap fillers like turnips and disguised them in green and brown bottles.

It was Henry Heinz who came up with the idea of putting his ketchup and horseradish in clear bottles so people could see what they were buying.

Heinz showed store-owners and consumers how pure and genuine his ketchup and horseradish were—and that was really the beginning of the Heinz food empire.

Heinz "sinks" competition

A real crisis hit the Heinz company.

There were three brothers who lived in Pittsburgh whose names were Fred, Jacob and Otto Heinz. They were not related to Henry Heinz. But they started a competing food company, made the same products as the original Heinz, and called their food "Heinz."

They also hired away the man who designed Henry's labels, making their products look virtually the same.

"You can't stop us," the three brothers wrote Henry. "We're just using our name, like you do."

Henry was beside himself. Consumers didn't know which Heinz product they were buying.

Today such a thing would probably bring an unfair-business lawsuit. But this was in the 1880s, not long after Henry Heinz began his company; and for reasons lost to history, Henry didn't sue. But he was upset, to put it mildly.

Then, fortune smiled on Henry. The three brothers couldn't pay their bank loans, and all their company assets were put up for sale. Henry went to the auction and bought everything—machinery, manufactured goods, containers, everything—and then Henry put all he could into a barge. He had that barge taken out to the middle of the Allegheny River in Pittsburgh, and sank it.

He literally sank his competition, and that was the end of the other Heinz company.

Man in a pickle
is saved by one

Henry Heinz found himself in a pickle at the Chicago World's Fair in 1893.

His Heinz food exhibit was in a poor location—on the second floor of a building at the far edge of the fairgrounds—and few people were coming to see it.

Not to be defeated, Henry hired boys to scatter notices around the fair telling people if they came to the Heinz exhibit, they would get a free gift.

Amazingly, over the next few days, thousands and thousands of people jammed the second floor for the gift. The floor became so crowded that officials at the fair were afraid it would collapse. They had to send workmen to shore up the floor. The free gift everybody came to get? The Heinz pickle pin. That was the start of one of the most famous giveaways in merchandising history.

Many companies give things away, but nothing has ever approached the impact, and the number, of pickle pins given away by Heinz.

In the years after that 1893 fair, Heinz gave away over 50 million pins. All over America it became sort of a badge of honor to wear the pickle pin. To use a current expression, young boys and girls thought it was cool to wear that pin.

Heinz became one of the first companies to get incredible free advertising with its name worn by so many people.

The pins have become a popular collectible—and are still in demand.

More than a century after Henry Heinz began his pickle pin idea, the company says it now gives away "about 57 pins every 30 minutes" to schools, conferences, clubs and the public at large.

(To order, see page 218)

A successful sales call
that salesmen can only dream of

Rarely has one sales call ever been so successful.

In 1886, Henry Heinz took his family on a trip to England.

As he was packing his luggage for the trip, Heinz put seven of his products in his Gladstone bag.

In London, he made a cold call on England's leading food purveyor. In those days, salesmen had to use a rear entrance, but Henry boldly walked in the front door and asked for the head man.

Heinz was in for two surprises. First, he luckily got to see the main buyer. Henry pulled his seven products out of his suitcase and asked the buyer to sample them. The second surprise?

To Henry's amazement, the man said, "We shall take them all."

With the distribution of those products in Britain, Heinz established his foothold in the U.K., and a special mutual love affair between the British people and Heinz products began. Today, Heinz is such a part of everyday life in Britain—from soup to beans—that many Britons argue Heinz is an English firm.

This one, cold sales call laid the groundwork for billions of dollars of revenues in the years since then.

They treat horses better than workers

It was a common saying in factories when the Industrial Revolution began in the 1800s that employers treated their horses better than their employees.

Women and children, especially, worked under deplorable conditions in what were called sweat shops. Long hours. Low pay. Few labor laws or unions. Benefits were almost unheard of.

Henry Heinz was always rebellious. In a then radical approach to employer-employee relations, he did just the opposite.

He didn't increase salaries above the norm of the times, but he pioneered employee benefits in American business. He provided free medical care with doctors, dentists and nurses on call at his factories.

He gave assembly-line workers free, clean clothes and indoor washrooms when most had no indoor plumbing at home.

He built gyms, swimming pools, libraries and auditoriums for his workers. During lunch hours in the men's and women's dining rooms, he had piano players and lecturers to entertain. Weekly free manicures were given to women food handlers.

In a final display of overcoming the horses-workers analogy, he used a hitch and a team of horses to drive employees, on a rotating basis, for lunch-time outings at public parks.

The pay wasn't so good

To realize how far factory workers have come, look at this payroll fact.

Women who worked at the Heinz factories in 1900 made 50 cents A DAY. And that was for a 10-hour day.

Working six days a week, as many did, employees took home the grand total of $3 each week for almost 60 hours of work.

But wait. In those days, it was common for factory workers to labor—not only 6 days a week—but also from 7 a.m. to 5:40 p.m. Henry Heinz made one concession, however. He let his employees go home at 4:40 p.m. on Saturdays.

Heinz paid NOT to have his products sold

In an odd switch, Henry Heinz was famous for "un-selling" his products.

Henry made regular visits to grocery stores. If he found aging Heinz products on the shelves, he paid grocers to remove them, took them back and destroyed them.

That wasn't his only reverse selling. Henry was an ardent non-drinker. His wife was a member of the Women's Christian Temperance Union, and he made trips to bars and saloons—not to drink but for another reason.

He didn't want his ketchup to be seen in a bar. He would walk in, gather up all his ketchup bottles, pay the saloon-keeper for them, and walk out with the bottles in his arms.

How Henry Heinz became rich

Early in his business career, Henry Heinz wrote down what he called Important Ideas and other mottoes. They helped him build, from the ground up, one of the biggest food empires in the world.

Among them was "A pure article of superior quality will find a ready market through its intrinsic value—if properly packaged and promoted."

Another was, "We keep our shingle out and then let the public blow our horn." (Heinz fervently believed in letting the public promote his name, and his Pickle Pin giveaway was—and is—one of the greatest promotions in history.)

His favorite motto was, "To do a common thing uncommonly well brings success."

For his employees, he had signs printed everywhere which said, "Do the best you can, where you are, with what you have today."

Long before many multinational companies existed, Heinz wrote, "The world is our field."

From his religious zeal came, "Quality is to a product what character is to a man. We are working for success and not for money. The money will take care of itself."

The energy of
Henry Heinz

Henry Heinz was, by all accounts, an unusually active man.

On his 71st birthday, an aide asked him how he felt reaching that age. Instead of answering, he jumped over a chair.

According to unofficial company historian Ed Lehew, Heinz was rarely at his desk. He seemingly was always on the go—traveling across the country and around the world.

Unlike many industrialists, he freely mingled with his employees on factory floors and in the fields where his products grew.

Henry was active in the company until his death in 1919, at age 75.

He had been head of the Heinz company for 50 years.

All in the family

Heinz is one of the rare multinational companies to have been headed by a father-son-grandson combination for 118 consecutive years.

Henry J. Heinz ran the company from its founding in 1869 until his death in 1919. His son, Howard, succeeded him; and Howard's son, Jack, took over in 1941 on Howard's death.

The string was broken when Jack's son, John, chose politics over business. John Heinz became a U.S. Senator from Pennsylvania and was still serving in the Senate when he was killed in a plane crash in 1991.

TWO

Catsup or Ketchup?

Two

Catsup or Ketchup?

Is it catsup, catchup or ketchup?

Just about everybody knows what ketchup is, but nobody—even word experts—can tell you what the "correct" spelling is.

Some dictionaries have favored "catsup," some say "ketchup," and some go with "catchup," or even "katsup."

A magazine writer once said, "Here's a sauce that can be pronounced by everybody—but spelled by nobody."

Oddly enough, the ORIGINAL spelling of this popular sauce was something else entirely.

So what is correct today? If you go by current usage, the No. 1 selling brand in the world is Heinz's "Ketchup."

But why do word experts still disagree about its spelling…

The Chinese had
the first word for it

There are two surprises about ketchup. Most Americans think ketchup is an American invention, and most think it has always been made with tomatoes.

Neither belief is true.

Ketchup was first used in China, and it was originally made from spiced fish—not tomatoes.

When the Chinese developed the tangy sauce over 300 years ago, they called it "ketsiap."

Its popularity spread to the Malay Peninsula where, in their local dialect, they named it "kechap."

Early in the 18th century, British sailors discovered it in Malaysia and brought samples back to England, where it began to be made with tomatoes.

It became widely popular in England. And English colonists brought it to America.

But the English didn't leave well enough alone with the spelling. For some unknown reason in those days, the English misspelled the sauce the Malaysians had called "kechap." The English added a "t" and made it "ketchup." And then…

**Everyone else
has the last word**

That should be the end of the story, but over the next 100 years or so, various writers and manufacturers couldn't resist playing around with the word "ketchup".

Some Anglicized the word further by changing the "k" to "c," making it "cetchup" and then "catchup."

One learned writer thought that was slang and campaigned for changing the name to "catsup," which he believed was the correct historic derivation. It turns out he probably didn't know about the original, authentic Asian spellings, which were closer to "ketchup."

The spelling of "catsup" was popular for a while, but today's spelling of "ketchup" is now more common. The Associated Press, for instance, now advises newspapers to use the spelling of "ketchup."

You can say that no popular food product has ever had so many different spellings.

What age group consumes the most ketchup?

It may surprise you to learn that the biggest consumers of ketchup are kids 6-to-12-years-old, followed closely by those 13 to 18.

The country in the world that buys the most ketchup on a per capita basis is Sweden, followed by Australia, the U.S., Canada and Germany.

The secret place to tap a bottle of ketchup

To release ketchup faster from the bottle, here's a little secret from the folks at Heinz:

They say the sweet spot to tap on the Heinz bottle is the "57" on the neck.

A survey by Heinz revealed that only 11 percent of people knew that secret; 21 percent vigorously shake the bottle; 20 percent thump the bottom and 29 percent use a knife.

All you need to do is apply a firm tap where the bottle narrows, and the ketchup will come out easier.

Another ketchup trick

There's another way to get ketchup out of the bottle more easily.

Put a drinking straw down to the bottom of the bottle.

The air channeled to the bottom from the straw allows the ketchup to pour.

What exactly is in ketchup?

The exact recipe for Heinz ketchup is closely guarded, but the ingredients are no secret.

Ketchup is made with a combination of cooked and strained tomatoes, plus vinegar, sugar or corn syrup, salt, onions, garlic, and a variety of natural spices.

The secret recipe

Although thousands of people work in factories making ketchup, Heinz officials say only 8 to 10 people know the exact recipe.

And, they guard that recipe as if it were a national security secret.

However, you may be surprised to learn that, although Heinz's basic recipe is constant, there are differences—depending in which country it's made.

One of the reasons for the success of Heinz ketchup worldwide is that they vary the flavor to satisfy local tastes.

For instance, consumers in England, Canada, Australia and Venezuela like their ketchup a bit sweeter than people in the U.S.

Mainland Europeans tend to like their ketchup spicier.

So, the main Heinz recipe for ketchup is the same—except for the slight background flavor of more or less spicing or sweetness.

If the Swedes do it, why can't Americans?

Most Americans don't put ketchup on their pasta; but in Sweden, that's a very popular custom.

That's just one example of how food habits vary among different nationalities. Bill Johnson, Heinz President and CEO—always looking for new ways to use food products—had an idea.

"It's just a matter of exposing different eating customs to different people—and that can be more easily accomplished in today's world through the Internet and other media," Johnson says.

Therefore, look for recipes that inspire you to try different uses for ketchup on your food products.

What product is in almost every home?

It's estimated that ketchup is in more than 90 percent of all homes in America. That's an astounding figure when you think about it.

Ketchup is easily one of the most-used products in the U.S. and around the world.

How much ketchup does Heinz sell?

More Heinz ketchup is sold around the world than any other brand.

They sell it in more than 140 countries, with annual sales of $1 billion.

That's more than twice the market share of their nearest competitor.

Heinz says if all of its ketchup sold in grocery stores were packaged in glass bottles and laid end to end, the bottles would circle the earth six times.

An incredible total of those little packets of ketchup

A unique part of Heinz's business is making packets of ketchup and dressings for restaurants.

The number of those packets Heinz makes each year is amazing, when you consider this:

The population of the entire world is about 6 billion people. Heinz sells 11 BILLION packets of ketchup—which means that's close to two packets for every person on earth.

Catsup or Ketchup?

Where
ketchup is free

Did you ever stop to think that when people go to a restaurant or fast-food place, they expect ketchup and other condiments to be free—representing, a significant expense for restaurant owners.

There was a small hamburger chain in Muscatine, Iowa that decided in 1970 to charge for ketchup. The cost was small—two pouches for five cents—but the backlash was so vehement, they dropped the idea after a month.

However, they soon went out of business because they were remembered as the restaurant that tried to charge for ketchup.

It wasn't fun making ketchup

As far back as the 18th century, ketchup was widely used—but people had to go to a lot of trouble to enjoy it.

It was mostly a homemade product then, and it was a time-consuming chore.

Homemakers had to peel tomatoes, make a sauce and constantly stir it while cooking. It often took people all day to make a batch of ketchup.

But help was on the way.

In 1876, Henry Heinz introduced the first mass-produced bottled ketchup to be sold in stores.

He advertised it as "Blessed relief for Mother and the other women in the household."

They agreed, and ketchup was on its way to becoming a product found almost everywhere.

A surprising health benefit from ketchup

For years, people have been using ketchup; and it's a good bet that most used it because it made food taste better—and not because they thought it was a special health food.

But new, independent studies by the University of Toronto and others conclude that consuming processed tomato products, like ketchup, may help to significantly raise levels of lycopene in the human body.

Lycopene is a powerful antioxidant that may aid in reducing the risk of certain cancers and heart disease.

It's found in fruits and vegetables—but the Toronto study found that lycopene from heat-processed tomatoes is more bioavailable than from fresh tomatoes. Heating tomatoes releases up to five times more lycopene than fresh tomatoes, making it easier for the body to absorb.

So because ketchup is made from cooked tomatoes, it turns out it's not only good, but good for you, too, based on these and other studies.

Ketchup is secret weapon at four-star restaurants

Although ketchup is the best-selling condiment in most countries of the world, you usually won't find bottles of it placed on tables in four-star restaurants.

However, *Food & Wine Magazine*, in a recent article, reports it has discovered that chefs at some of New York's best restaurants see ketchup as their secret weapon.

Jean-Georges Vongerichten of Jean Georges combines it with soy sauce, vinegar and butter to make a silky sauce for cod.

At Lespinasse, Christian Delouvier sauces pork with a blend of ketchup, soy sauce and honey because he likes the complex sweet and tangy flavors.

David Waltuck at Chanterelle makes a sweet ginger—and ketchup—spiked sauce that he uses for everything from dipping onion fritters to glazing crisp chicken thighs.

The magazine says more and more four-star chefs have become fascinated by humble ketchup and are using it in some of their most sublime recipes.

Catsup or Ketchup?

Tomatoes for ketchup never touched by human hands

Years ago when a company wanted to make a product like ketchup, the tomatoes were all picked by hand—and then, again, touched by hands during the processing.

Today, with mechanization by companies like Heinz, the tomatoes are never touched—even in picking them from the fields.

Mechanical harvesters now pick tomatoes. The harvesters are so advanced they have "color discriminators" that automatically select only red, ripe tomatoes, kicking out green tomatoes, mud, etc.

The good tomatoes are dropped into trucks that take them to factories where they are sterilized by heat and processed into ketchup—all without human hands ever touching them.

While the ingredients are being sterilized in one location, the bottles are sterilized a short distance away; and then the ketchup is put into the bottles and sealed, again by automation.

Psychologist uncovers amazing fact about ketchup eaters

Dr. Paul Rozin, a psychology professor at the University of Pennsylvania, studies people's eating habits.

He says people, generally, don't like to work when they eat; and therefore he's amazed at the lengths people will go to get ketchup out of a Heinz bottle.

"Consumers' habits are unique, almost playful when it comes to the Heinz ketchup bottle," Dr. Rozin says. "They are willing to invest the time to get the ketchup out, forestalling the pleasure of eating."

"Ketchup is one of the few constants in our culture. It's fascinating how strongly people feel about this condiment—not only experiencing its flavor, but also working to get it from the bottle," Dr. Rozin concludes.

Ketchup "graduates" to plastic

In the famous 1967 movie, "The Graduate," Dustin Hoffman, playing a recent college graduate about to enter the business world, is told that the big word for the future is "plastics."

Whether someone at Heinz was influenced by that line in the movie is unknown, but the fact is Bill Johnson, who became Heinz President and CEO, led a long period of development to put ketchup in a squeezable, less-breakable plastic container.

It took 15 years of testing before Heinz found the right combination of technology for a multilayer plastic bottle that met the needs of the consumer and maintained the quality and integrity of the product at the right price.

Heinz beat their competitors by 18 months in coming out with ketchup in the squeezable plastic container. Kids and their parents loved it and it took the market by storm. The year was 1983, and it revolutionized grocery ketchup, giving Heinz a commanding lead in sales.

Whether in plastic or the classic glass bottle, Heinz still sells more ketchup, by far, than any other company in the world.

Fun facts
about ketchup

- The world's largest ketchup bottle is a water tower in Collinsville, Illinois, that stands 170 feet tall.
- U.S. President Richard Nixon refused to eat cottage cheese without ketchup.
- The average bottles of ketchup each American consumes in a year is three.
- Olympic champion gymnast Nadia Comaneci would eat only food with ketchup when she first came to the U.S.
- Food fads come and go, but ketchup was America's No. 1 condiment in the 1800s, and still is today.
- According to a recent survey, the food most people would refuse to eat without ketchup is meatloaf.

THREE

The StarKist Story

Three

The StarKist Story

It doesn't say "Heinz," but it is Heinz's

For almost the first 100 years of Heinz's history, their products all carried the Heinz name.

But in 1963, that changed.

Heinz bought another family-run company—StarKist, and today Heinz makes and sells StarKist food under the StarKist brand.

The beginnings of the StarKist company are amazingly similar to Heinz's.

Both were started from scratch by men who had no formal business education. From the humblest of beginnings, they built giant food companies, were succeeded by their sons, and their brands are household names today.

Heinz's StarKist subsidiary is now the world's largest processor of canned seafood, and here's how it all began...

One man—in one boat— launched a billion-dollar food empire

In 1910, a recent immigrant, Martin Bogdanovich, bought a boat and set out to catch fish off the shores of San Pedro, California.

No one then could have predicted that Bogdanovich and his one little fishing boat would lead to the best-known and most popular brand of canned tuna in the world.

Bogdanovich's simple beginning was the start of a gigantic operation. He eventually did more than just catch fish. He formed a family company that processed and packaged it. Years later, his son, Joe, came up with the name StarKist.

Tuna is popular both for its taste and nutrition. Amazingly today, almost 90 percent of U.S. families buy tuna on a regular basis. It is America's No. 1 fish.

How StarKist
got its name

When Martin Bogdanovich started his company, his tuna didn't have a brand name of its own.

His company was, oddly enough, called The French Sardine Co. That's because they originally caught sardines as well as tuna. But schools of sardines mysteriously disappeared from what were once rich fishing waters, and Bogdanovich and others then concentrated on tuna.

They found tuna was plentiful—and more important, they discovered people enjoyed it.

When Martin's son, Joe, became active in the company, he thought their tuna should have its own brand, although Martin didn't think it was necessary.

Along came a former food broker, Barney Tast, who met with Joe Bogdanovich and talked about ways they could increase their tuna sales.

Tast agreed with Joe that the tuna needed a brand name; and since he used to work for the White Star brokerage firm in Salt Lake City, Utah, he suggested the word "Star" and said why not have a kissing couple on the label and call the brand StarKist. Joe liked the name, but not the kissing couple.

The StarKist label—without the kissing

couple—first appeared on cans of tuna in 1942.

The company capitalized on the name "Star," by using Hollywood stars to endorse the product in a "Tuna of the Stars" advertising campaign. It helped put StarKist on the national map.

Today, Charlie the Tuna stands between the words "Star" and "Kist" on the labels.

How Charlie the Tuna was born

To have a symbol for their tuna, StarKist decided it wanted something like Tony the Tiger®, the Pillsbury Doughboy® or the Jolly Green Giant®, and so they turned to the advertising agency that created all those characters, the Leo Burnett Co.

A Burnett employee, Tom Rogers, invented Charlie the Tuna. He modeled him after a cool street guy he remembered who used to hang out in a drug store in Rogers' hometown of New York City.

Rogers made Charlie look like a 1960s hipster with a cap and sunglasses, talking about how it was a "status thing" to be picked by StarKist.

For Charlie's New York voice, Rogers chose actor Herschel Bernardi.

Charlie made his national TV debut in 1962.

Sorry, Charlie

The classic line, "Sorry, Charlie," that many people use (even when they're not talking to somebody named Charlie), came from this television commercial.

The commercial featured Charlie the Tuna and his unsuccessful attempts to be chosen for StarKist tuna.

He was rejected every time, triggering the line, "Sorry, Charlie."

What is albacore tuna?

You often see the word "albacore" on cans of tuna. Here's what that means:

Albacore is one species of tuna fish. It is the only all-white-meat kind of tuna.

It's a firm, delicately mild fish found in temperate waters around the world. Albacore caught for canning vary in size from 9 to 70 pounds. But it is the rarest kind of commercially popular tuna. Albacore apparently are fewer in number than other tuna, and the annual catch is relatively limited.

Other
tunas

The other types of popular tuna are yellowfin and the skipjack.

Yellowfin is rich and flavorful, taken from warm, tropical waters. This light-meat species ranges in size from 10 to more than 200 pounds; however, the 30-to-70-pound fish are considered the choicest for canning.

The skipjack is the world's most abundant species of tuna and is harvested from virtually all equatorial waters. Skipjacks range from 4 to 24 pounds, making them the smallest light-meat pieces.

Although tuna live in tropical and subtropical waters in all parts of the world, they venture as far north as Newfoundland and Norway in the Atlantic and British Columbia and Northern Japan in the Pacific in summer months.

Why tuna became so popular

A few years after Martin Bogdanovich started catching tuna from his one fishing boat off the California coast, World War I began—and with it came meat shortages.

The U.S. government was looking for new sources of protein to help replace the protein lost in people's meat diets. They were also looking for a versatile, nutritious, good-tasting food for the troops.

Canned tuna was a perfect answer.

The new, ready market for tuna allowed Bogdanovich to hire more fishermen and build his first cannery, starting the future StarKist company on its way.

Tuna remained popular after World War I, and then got another impetus when meat rationing during World War II again turned more consumers and the government to the high-protein and nutritious values of tuna fish.

It turns out that tuna is richer in protein than beef, is high in vitamins, low in calories and cholesterol and, therefore, has been called a perfect food.

The incredible work needed to make a can of tuna

The can of tuna in your supermarket looks like a simple thing—but the amount of time and work to produce that can is amazing.

Fleets of ships must spend many days roaming the oceans to find the tuna in the first place. Then the tuna have to be caught.

Once on board the StarKist ships, the tuna are sent down a wet chute into refrigerated compartments where they are frozen in brine.

When the ships dock, a series of labor-intensive jobs begins. For StarKist, this is an enormous job since they are the world's largest tuna processor.

The tuna are separated by size and shape and loaded into bins. Samples are taken to a Department of Agriculture lab for tests that measure levels of mercury, salt, nitrate, water, oil and fat.

Next, the fish are thawed in fresh water, cut, and washed, then steamed, tested for aroma, cooled by a computerized mist system for several hours and hand filleted.

No part of the fish is wasted. Some portions are used for pet food, animal feed, fish oil and fertilizer.

Finally, the fillets of tuna destined for human consumption are canned and vacuum packed. The cans are given a final sterilization, sealed, cooled, labeled, and sent off to stores with an eight-digit code that tells who caught the fish and where, when it was processed and packed, and the date the can was sealed.

All that for a little can of tuna.

FOUR

Incredible Vinegar

Four

Incredible Vinegar

Can you think of any food product that has more uses than vinegar?

In sports, they give awards for a "Most Valuable Player." If there were a "Most Valuable Food" award, vinegar would have to be a leading candidate.

Vinegar has been used for medicinal purposes. It was one of the first antibiotics known. Today, it's used for rashes, bites and other similar minor ailments. And some people say they get health benefits by drinking a small amount of vinegar.

It's also useful as a helper for many household chores.

And, for hundreds of years, cooks have used vinegar to flavor food, and for pickling and preserving.

Incredible cooking tips
with white vinegar

There are an amazing number of tricks you can use with white vinegar to help make meal preparation better and easier.

Researchers at Heinz say by using their white vinegar you can:

- Revive wilted vegetables. Soak them in one quart of cold water and a tablespoon of white vinegar.
- Make rice less sticky and easier to spoon out. Add a teaspoon of white vinegar to the boiling water.
- Rescue a recipe that's too sweet or salty. Add a dash of white vinegar.
- Put more gel in gelatin. When temperatures rise, molded salads and desserts will stand up to the heat if you add a teaspoon of white vinegar per box of gelatin.
- Enhance flavor of grilled fish. Add a dash of white vinegar. For firmer, whiter fish, soak for 20 minutes in one quart of water and two tablespoons of vinegar.

- Make buttermilk. If a recipe calls for buttermilk, and you don't have any, add a tablespoon of white vinegar to a cup of milk. Let it stand for five minutes to thicken, and you've created buttermilk.
- Prevent hard-boiled eggs from cracking and have the shells peel off faster and easier. Add two tablespoons of white vinegar per quart of water before boiling.
- Tenderize tough meats and game. A mixture of one-half cup of white vinegar added to a cup of liquid bouillon makes a great marinade base.
- Keep cheese fresh and free of mold. Wrap it in a cloth saturated with white vinegar and store airtight in the refrigerator.

Incredible household tips with white vinegar

Just as white vinegar is good for many cooking tips, it can also help in an amazing number of household chores.

The Vinegar Institute lists some ways white vinegar can make your household work easier.

Incredible Vinegar

Use white vinegar to:

- Cut soapy film on cloudy glassware in the dishwasher. Place a cup of white vinegar on the bottom rack of the dishwasher, run for five minutes, then run through the full cycle. A cup of white vinegar run through the full cycle once a month will also reduce soap buildup on the inside of the machine.
- Make chrome fixtures, appliance surfaces and countertops gleam. Rub away streaks and smears with a cloth soaked in white vinegar.
- Prevent grease buildup and keep drains fresh-smelling. Pour a handful of baking soda down the drainpipe. Add one-half cup of white vinegar. Cover the drain tightly for a few minutes, then flush with cold water.
- Remove food stains from pots and pans. Soak the insides of pots and pans in full-strength white vinegar for 30 minutes. Then rinse in hot, soapy water.
- Clean toilet bowl. Pour in one cup of undiluted white vinegar. Let stand for five minutes, then flush.

- Get rid of unpleasant odors. For onion odors: Rub some white vinegar on your fingers before and after slicing onions to eliminate lingering after-aroma. To absorb stale, smoky smells, a bowl of vinegar placed in an out-of-the-way corner of any room works wonders. To get rid of fishy smells, boil a tablespoon of white vinegar in a cup of water.
- To keep garbage disposal clean and fresh-smelling, make some vinegar ice cubes. Mix one cup of vinegar in enough water to fill an ice tray, freeze the mixture, then grind the cubes through the disposal and flush with cold water.
- Remove lime deposit corrosion from showerheads. Soak in a container filled with full-strength white vinegar overnight.
- Get rid of bathtub and tile film. Wipe with vinegar and rinse with water.
- Eliminate mildew and grimy buildup on shower curtains. Use full-strength vinegar to wipe it away, or place shower and bath curtains in washing machine, along with a bath towel. Add one cup of white vinegar during the rinse cycle. Dry on low for three minutes.

- Have soft, shiny hair. After shampooing, rinse hair well with one cup of water and a tablespoon of white vinegar.
- Clean bathroom floors. Use a solution of one-half cup of white vinegar and one gallon of water to mop tile or linoleum. For tough stains, apply undiluted white vinegar directly on the stain.
- Make smoky or other unpleasant odors vanish from clothes. Pour two cups of vinegar in a bathtub of hot water, hang the clothes above the tub, and let the odors disappear.
- Remove unsightly hem marks that remain after altering hemlines. Rub them away with a white vinegar-dampened cloth. Then run a steam iron across the crease or tell-tale line.
- Get rid of light scorch marks or stains left by underarm deodorants on fabrics. Rub lightly with undiluted white vinegar, then wipe with a clean cloth.
- Freshen up the washing machine. Once a month, pour in a cup of white vinegar. Run through a normal cycle, without clothes, and unwanted soap residue will vanish.

- Bring up the color and nap in carpets and rugs. Brush with a mixture of one cup of white vinegar per gallon of water, then blot dry.
- Clean and deodorize pet stains. Pour undiluted vinegar on stain, wipe clean with strong strokes, then blot the area with cold water.
- Keep exhaust fan grills, ceiling fan blades and air conditioning grills dust-free and circulating fresh air. Wipe them with full-strength white vinegar to cut grease and dirt.
- Extend the life of flowers in your house. Add two tablespoons of white vinegar plus three tablespoons of sugar per quart of warm water. Cut flowers will bloom longer. Stems should be in three to four inches of the water.
- End streaky windows. Use vinegar full strength in a spray bottle and wash streaks and film away.
- Take the sting out of sunburn. Sponge on vinegar to soothe skin.

- Renew varnished woodwork and furniture. Rub with a soft cloth moistened with a solution of one tablespoon of white vinegar in a quart of lukewarm water. Buff up with a soft, dry cloth. Tell-tale white rings from wet glasses will disappear by rubbing them with a mixture of equal parts of olive oil and white vinegar.
- Rescue shoes from damaging effects of salt stains. Pour undiluted white vinegar on a damp cloth and wipe into the affected areas. Then polish with a soft cloth.
- Kill unwanted grass and weeds in sidewalk cracks and on driveways. Pour on full-strength vinegar.
- Loosen rusty bolts and stubborn spigots. Soak them in full-strength white vinegar.
- Remove unwanted decals and bumper stickers. Wipe them repeatedly with white vinegar. Let the vinegar soak in. In a few minutes, the decals should peel off easily.
- Avoid ice on a car's windshield. If you leave car out overnight in winter, coat the windows with a solution of three parts white or cider vinegar to one part water.

How vinegar got its name

The name vinegar comes from the French word "vinaigre"—"vin" for wine and "aigre" for sour—and was called sour wine, although many vinegars are made without wine.

Vinegar is one of the oldest food products in history—and one of the most versatile. It was used by the Babylonians as far back as 5,000 B.C.

Ancient people used vinegar to add taste to food and for steeping vegetables; marinating meat; making pickles; preserving herbs, vegetables and flowers; and even purifying water and as a reliable cleaning agent.

It was also one of the first medicines. Hippocrates, the father of medicine, used vinegar as an antibiotic in 400 B.C. During the U.S. Civil War, vinegar was used to prevent scurvy among soldiers; in World War I, it was used to treat wounds.

With all that, you'd think somebody would have bottled it—and someone finally did.

Vinegar—the wonder product—
finally reaches homes
the easy way

For thousands of years, people found many uses for vinegar—but they couldn't go to the store and buy a bottle of it.

People often kept barrels of vinegar in their cellars in the old days, and many made it themselves.

Even the great food marketer, Henry Heinz, didn't sell individual bottles of vinegar at first. He manufactured vinegar to preserve the appearance and flavor of his pickles, and it was a necessary ingredient of his ketchup and other condiments—but he didn't put it on sale.

That all changed in the late 1800s when Heinz became America's first manufacturer to package vinegar in individual bottles for home use.

Today, there's a large variety of vinegars—and an estimated 90 percent of all households buy it.

How many kinds
of vinegar are there?

Vinegar can be made from any fruit or from any material containing natural sugar.

Among the most popular kinds of vinegar are those made from apple juice, grapes, peaches and berries, in addition to vinegar made with wine.

Malt vinegar uses barley malt or other cereals.

Sugar vinegar can come from different types of syrups or molasses.

Spirit or distilled vinegar is, as you might guess, made from alcohol.

Labels on bottles of vinegar describe the starting ingredients, such as "apple cider vinegar" or "wine vinegar," etc.

Vinegar lasts…and lasts…and lasts

According to studies by the Vinegar Institute, the shelf life of vinegar is almost indefinite.

Because of its acid nature, vinegar is self-preserving and does not need refrigeration.

White vinegar will remain virtually unchanged over a long period of time. While some changes can be seen in other types of vinegar, such as a color change or the development of a haze or sediment, this is only an aesthetic change. The product can still be used with confidence.

FIVE

Ore-Ida Saga

Five

Ore-Ida Saga

How little Ore-Ida
became big and popular

The Ore-Ida saga is the classic story of a small, regional company's products evolving into national recognition.

It started in 1951 when two brothers, Nephi and Golden Grigg, mortgaged their homes to buy an old frozen food factory in Ontario, Oregon.

Nephi Grigg was the driving force in the business. Much like Heinz founder, Henry Heinz, Nephi began his business career as a teenager, raising corn and selling it door-to-door, using a horse and wagon. One of 13 children in a Mormon family, he never went beyond the 10th grade.

He and his brother, Golden, processed their first french-fried potatoes in 1952 and then developed a wasted by-product into one of their most famous and popular brands.

Ore-Ida Saga

They took the slivers of potatoes left over from making french fries, ground them, mixed them with spices, cooked them in oil, and produced a new treat, Tater Tots.

But Ore-Ida was still a small family business. The brothers called on accounts—with briefcases filled with dry ice to carry their frozen foods.

The company grew, and Heinz, looking for acquisitions, bought it 14 years after the Grigg brothers started it. Heinz was able to provide the advertising, marketing and manufacturing know-how that propelled Ore-Ida into a major brand.

The slogan that boosted Ore-Ida

Ore-Ida products were popular when Heinz took them over, but their name didn't have big brand awareness around America.

Heinz spent $15 million on TV and in women's magazines advertising Ore-Ida in 1978 and hired the Doyle Dane Bernbach agency to come up with a slogan.

The slogan, "When it says it's Ore-Ida, it's all-righta," solidified the brand name, and Ore-Ida became the No. 1 frozen-food item in the U.S.

Why are those products called Ore-Ida?

All the products that have the brand Ore-Ida got their name from two neighboring U.S. states, Oregon and Idaho.

The original Ore-Ida company was based in Ontario, Oregon, and Burley, Idaho, so they took the "Ore" from Oregon and the "Ida" from Idaho.

Ore-Ida was purchased by the Heinz company in 1965.

The amount of popular potato products they sell today is staggering.

For instance, one Ore-Ida plant produces enough french fries every day that, if placed end-to-end would reach from Canada to Mexico.

That's their production EVERY DAY.

Pizza on a bagel?

Pizza was first made in Naples, Italy, in the 1700s. A baker to the royal court created it; but unfortunately, this ingenious cook's name is lost in history.

Those in the royal court loved it, and its popularity spread to the commoners in Italy.

Interestingly, pizza's widespread use in America didn't begin until after World War II, when servicemen and women who had fought in Italy brought home the demand for it.

Pizza literally means "pie" in Italian—but now consumers can get pizza toppings, not just on a pizza pie, but on a bagel.

Ore-Ida makes frozen Bagel Bites, which are really mini-pizzas. They're bagels with choices of three cheeses, red and green peppers, pepperoni and tomato sauce.

Bagel Bites are an interesting marriage of the Jewish bagel with the Italian pizza.

How bagels got their name

The word "bagel" comes from Yiddish, which in turn has an old German derivation from the word meaning "bracelet."

For years, bagels were eaten primarily by European Jews and could be found in the U.S. only in New York and a few other big cities.

Bagels were largely unknown by the general population until some 20 years ago. What was once an ethnic food is now widely popular, as is the case with so many others, like tacos and pizza.

French fries NOT from France

You would think that french fried potatoes got their name because they originated in France. But such is not the case.

Most food historians believe french fries were first made by little shops in Liege, Belgium.

Their popularity spread to nearby France and then to the rest of the world under the wrong name of "french" fried.

How many potatoes
do Americans eat?

It may surprise you to know that the average American eats over 130 pounds of potatoes a year in every form, from baked to fried.

Potatoes are to Americans what canned beans are to the British—a regular, favorite food.

The leading brand of frozen potatoes in the U.S. is Ore-Ida, with its Tater Tots brand, Golden Twirls brand, Crispers brand, mashed potatoes, twice baked, shoestring, hash browns, and other varieties.

Ore-Ida is one of the strongest consumer franchises in America, with perhaps more brand loyalty than any other Heinz product, except ketchup.

Besides being No. 1 in U.S. supermarkets in frozen potato products, Ore-Ida also makes stuffed pasta, coated vegetables and frozen appetizers.

By the way, to satisfy American appetites for potatoes, Ore-Ida's potato volume is about one billion pounds a year.

Things you never knew
about potatoes

The famous Irish potato is not Irish at all.

Potatoes originated in South America and were unknown in the rest of the world until European explorers discovered them in the 1500s in Peru, Colombia and Bolivia.

The explorers brought potatoes to North America and Europe—and because potatoes grew especially well in Irish soil, they emerged as the main crop in Ireland.

That's how the transported white potato became known as the Irish potato.

But disaster struck. The Irish, who grew increasingly dependent on each year's crop, faced a devastating depression in 1845 and 1846 when the nation's potato production failed because of a spreading plant disease.

Thousands of Irish people died of starvation or migrated to the U.S., setting up a huge wave of Irish immigration to America.

Today, potatoes are one of the most widely

grown vegetables on earth. Billions of bushels are produced each year to feed the world's desire for french fries and baked, boiled and mashed potatoes.

By the way, surprisingly, the sweet potato is not related to the potato, according to botanists. Potatoes belong to the nightshade family, genus Solanum. Sweet potatoes are classified in the morning-glory family, genus Ipomoea.

SIX

Surprising Food Facts

Six

Surprising Food Facts

How hot dogs
got their name

Hot dogs were invented at a baseball game in New York in the early 1900s.

It was a cool day, and the concessionaire, Harry Stevens, wasn't selling much cold food—which was all they had at games in those days.

Harry went shopping for something warm he could sell. Stevens bought sausage at a neighborhood butcher shop, but the problem was: how could fans at the game hold the sausages?

Stevens added buns—and the hot dog was born, but it didn't have its name yet.

A well-known sports cartoonist, Tad Dorgan, was at the game. He drew a picture for the next day's newspaper showing a dachshund in a bun. The shape of the sausage reminded him of a dachshund, but for the title of the cartoon, he had trouble spelling "dachshund." So he settled for "Hot Dog"—and the name was coined.

No ham in hamburgers

Since there's no ham in hamburgers, why are they called hamburgers?

To answer that question, you have to go back to the late 1800s, when a group of people came to the U.S. from Hamburg, Germany.

They brought with them a new custom— serving ground meat.

That kind of meat was soon named after their town—Hamburg. And that's how hamburgers got their name.

On what days do Americans eat the most food?

Super Bowl Sunday is now the second-biggest day for food consumption in homes, according to a survey by Hallmark cards.

The survey says that Super Bowl Sunday has surpassed the previous No. 2, New Year's Eve, for most at-home eating.

Remaining in the No. 1 position is Thanksgiving Day.

How worcestershire sauce got its complicated name

A British nobleman, Sir Marcus Sandys, became the governor of a province in India in the mid-1800s.

While there, he acquired the recipe for a tangy sauce made from a secret blend of spices and seasonings.

He returned to his estate in England, which was located in the town of Worcester. Sandys had bottles of the sauce prepared for his private use and for gifts to friends.

Its popularity prompted Sandys to license manufacturers to make the sauce commercially under the name of Worcester Sauce, in honor of his home town.

When the product debuted in America, its name was changed to Worcestershire—the word "shire" being the British equivalent of county. Worcestershire is the county where Worcester is located.

Americans found it easy to enjoy the sauce, if not the pronunciation and spelling of the name.

From "poison" to "passion": the strange story of the tomato

Surprisingly, when European explorers first came to America, they had never seen tomatoes before. Tomatoes then grew only in the Americas.

· The explorers took seeds back to Europe, where they raised tomatoes for decoration.

Then the strange story of the tomato started.

For years, many people thought tomatoes were poisonous and they were never eaten. On the other hand, a rumor arose among some that tomatoes had special qualities which stimulated love—and they were called "love apples."

In any case, the vast majority of people never ate or used tomatoes until they finally became a popular food in the mid-1800s.

The once-thought-to-be-strange tomato is today known as a good source of vitamins A and C, with other health benefits, to say nothing of its versatility as a food product.

Don't squeeze the tomato

To completely mechanize the process from picking to manufacturing tomato products, one of the neatest tricks is putting 13 tons of tomatoes in a truck, without crushing the ones on the bottom.

After those tomatoes are mechanically harvested in the fields, they are loaded into trucks and taken as far as 400 miles to the factory.

If tomatoes are smashed, they're useless in the manufacturing and sterilization process.

Heinz solved the problem by breeding a special strain of tomatoes that have a thick skin and are fleshy enough NOT to be crushed on the trip to the factory.

Employees say those tomatoes are so firm you can throw them against a wall and not damage them.

As the old saying goes, "Those are some tomatoes."

What's the difference between jelly and jam?

Most jelly is made by boiling fruit. The cooked fruit is then put in a special bag that allows the juices to drip through to large containers.

The juice is then mixed with sugar and boiled until it "jells" or congeals. From "jell" comes the name "jelly."

The thing that makes the juice jell is pectin. Many fruits have a natural abundance of pectin. For those that do not, pectin is added from other fruits.

Jams are made much the same way, except the juice is not drained off. The juice AND pulp from the fruit are kept together to make jam.

"Cool as a cucumber"

Although many foods can be served cold, here's why the cucumber led to the expression "cool as a cucumber."

Cucumbers were first grown in the hot climates of Southern Asia.

Popular folklore there said that cucumbers had a special cooling effect on people—and the expression was born.

Why is it called "mayonnaise"?

Mayonnaise was first made on the Spanish island of Minorca in the Mediterranean Sea.

The major port city of Minorca is Mahon, and it became famous in Europe for its delicious sauce, then called "Mahon" sauce.

French tourists brought the recipe back to France where chefs used it for the best meats and renamed it "mahonnaise."

When it spread to the rest of Europe and America in the early 1800s, it was considered a delicate French creation.

Its popularity grew to where it's now used on all kinds of foods, and the English-speaking world changed the spelling, substituting a "y" for the "h" and making the former, exotic Mahon "mahonnaise" sauce—"mayonnaise."

Many food products don't make it

It's estimated that over 20,000 new grocery products are introduced in supermarkets every year.

Because stores can only display a certain number of items, room must be made for both the new products as well as the existing ones.

Stores keep careful track of which products consumers are buying and which ones they are not. Sales of products are usually tracked on a daily or weekly basis.

Because shelf space is limited, it is tough for many of those 20,000 new products each year to make it—but, on the other hand, it is just as difficult for existing brands to stay alive.

Therefore, it's amazing when you look at a product like Heinz Ketchup. It was in stores over 120 years ago, and it is still there—basically the same as it was in 1876. Very few brands last that long.

Here's why we call accountants 'bean counters'

You often hear the expression "bean counters" applied to accountants, and the funny thing is the origin of that name came from accountants actually counting real beans.

Canned beans are very popular in England, and Heinz's U.K. division was running a special promotion on its beans.

To determine what their inventory was, the company sent out a group of their accountants to literally count the number of cans of beans in various stores.

When the accountants got back to the main office, other employees in the company started referring to them as "bean counters"—and the name stuck, and spread.

The soup mystery

One of the surprises in supermarkets is that while Heinz soups are the most popular brand in countries like Britain and Australia, just the reverse is true in the United States and Canada.

While they've had spectacular success with ketchup, StarKist, Ore-Ida, and many other products in North America, Heinz has made it with soups under their own name only for a short time. (Heinz does make a large number of successful private-label soups.)

It's a mystery why Heinz-brand soup has not become popular on its home continent. And it hasn't been for the lack of trying.

Jack Heinz, the company's chief executive, went on television himself in 1963 and was seen in print ads promoting Heinz soups. He was one of the first corporate leaders to do that, pre-dating Lee Iacocca of Chrysler® and Dave Thomas of Wendy's®.

The mystery deepened because Heinz's soups were considered excellent by people in the industry.

Products like Happy Soup for children and Great American Soups followed, but failed.

Heinz U.S.A. then exited the retail soup business, and it turned out to be a good profit-loss decision because they moved on to making the private-label soups which, with no advertising costs, are hugely successful.

Today, Heinz makes more than 80 percent of all private-label soups, and it has become their second-biggest business after ketchup. They make over 50 varieties of soups under 140 different labels.

That's a lot of tomatoes

What company buys more tomatoes than any other company in the world? The answer? Heinz. They buy over two million TONS a year.

All those tomatoes are used in ketchup and several hundred other tomato-based products, such as sauces, pastas, juices, purees, beans, chili, etc.

The wonders of garlic

Garlic, used in condiments like ketchup and many other foods, has had a tremendous variety of properties attributed to it.

The ancient Romans gave it to laborers to make them stronger, and to soldiers to give them courage.

In the Middle Ages, it was used to ward off disease and evil spirits, and its antiseptic qualities were thought to be a good defense against the plague.

Today, crushed garlic applied to the skin helps fight insect bites and stings.

Farmers find uses for garlic, such as planting it around peach trees to stop destruction by peach borers.

There are people who believe garlic has an antibiotic that can fight colds; it also has a reputation of lowering blood pressure.

Some qualities about garlic are folklore, some are real—but with or without its medicinal uses, it is a popular flavoring for food.

Why do we say

"barbecue?"

Originally, barbecue referred to the roasting of a whole hog, ox or other large animal on a rack—and the word "barbecue" came from the French "barbe" or whiskers and "queue" or tail. In other words, the animal was roasted from whiskers to tail.

The French are credited with introducing this method of cooking in other countries.

Today, barbecue usually refers to any meat basted with or served in a barbecue sauce. The sauce traditionally has a combination of such ingredients as onions, garlic, ketchup, vinegar and spices.

And, we've changed the spelling from the old French to different variations like bar-b-que and in Heinz's case, to B-B-Q sauce.

Barbecued meat is now roasted on a revolving spit, or a grid, over coals or in an oven.

SEVEN

For Cats and Dogs

Seven

For Cats and Dogs

Dogs & cats didn't have their own food

In the old days, pets, like cats and dogs, didn't have food or treats made especially for them.

Before the mass-marketing of pet foods, household pets got table scraps and leftovers from food their owners ate.

But pets have special diet needs, different from humans, so the pet food industry has made for generally healthier animals.

Today's good commercial dog and cat food is specially designed to provide complete and balanced nutrition for pet growth and maintenance.

An unusual group of eaters

How do manufacturers of pet foods decide what products cats and dogs will like; and, therefore, what products to make or improve?

They turn to the experts—and in this case the "experts" at Heinz, for example, are a collection of dogs and cats at a highly supervised, well-maintained kennel in California.

This test "panel" of animals is used to judge the food that their fellow dogs and cats everywhere will be eating in the future.

During the feeding studies, officials at the kennel observe if the animals have to be coaxed to eat the food, or if they really like it.

A large collection of different varieties and breeds of dogs and cats live in "luxury" at the kennel.

The food tests include animals of different ages since specific foods are targeted to puppies and kittens as well as to middle-aged and older pets.

All in all, it doesn't sound like a bad job for a dog or cat.

What's in a name?

It's too bad cats and dogs can't read the names on the brands of some of their food.

The people who make and sell pet food must spend hours thinking of names that people might enjoy, even though their pets can't read them.

The folks at Heinz came up with dog food and treats brands named Pup-Peroni, Wagwells, Jerky Treats, Skippy, Meaty Bone, Gravy Train, Ken-L-Ration, Reward, Grill Stix, Kibbles'n Bits and Snausages.

For cats, besides the famous 9-Lives, there's Amore and Pounce.

In South Africa, there's Catz-D-Lite and Dogz-D-Lite.

Pet food has become a multibillion-dollar industry—and it continues to grow, fueled by an increasing singles population and an aging "empty nest" population seeking companionship of a pet. People are also having fewer children and acquiring pets as surrogates.

Morris the Cat
was real

StarKist wanted to come up with a "spokesperson" for their 9-Lives cat food.

As they did for Charlie the Tuna, StarKist turned to the Leo Burnett Advertising Agency, who found a cat in an animal shelter—and named him Morris.

Morris went on national TV for the first time in 1969.

He had an independent attitude and finicky ways that cat lovers appreciated. Morris gave the message that even the most finicky cat would be pleased with 9-Lives cat food.

When the first Morris died, the advertising agency could have quietly replaced him; but instead, they embarked on a national search for a new "Morris."

Inter-office memo
makes national news

When the first Morris the Cat died, Heinz circulated an "obituary" for Morris around the office—never thinking it would go public.

But someone tipped off the media, and it was picked up by national TV and newspapers across America.

Much to the surprise of people at Heinz, it became a big story, as fans of Morris everywhere expressed their sympathy.

The first Morris was replaced in the 9-Lives cat food commercials by another stray cat found in an animal shelter, and Heinz decided to always use cats from shelters whenever they need to "retire" a Morris.

Why do we say cats have 9 lives?

The familiar saying—cats have nine lives—gave birth to the name of a popular cat food, but why do we say cats have nine lives?

According to word experts, it's a combination of mythology plus some realistic observations.

In Egyptian mythology, there was a cat-headed goddess named Bast, and she was said to possess nine lives—nine being a mystical number in those days. Because the cat-goddess supposedly had nine lives, the saying was extended to cats themselves.

The saying was fortified over the years by the fact that cats are seen to have strong self-preservation. Cats always seem to land on their feet and have paws that are well-padded and shock-absorbing. Cats also seem good at taking care of themselves.

So the myth of cats having nine lives grew, and continues today.

Unlikely person names 9-Lives

9-Lives cat food is a No. 1 brand—and it has a great name for cats.

But, that name wasn't suggested by an advertising or marketing person, as is usually the case.

When StarKist was deciding what to call its cat food, the name 9-Lives was suggested by, of all people, a company lawyer.

We assume he enjoyed the necessary, ensuing trademark search and registration of the name he created.

Nutritional tips for pets

Specific tips for dogs and cats are listed in the two following items; but for all pets, it's a good idea to check with your veterinarian for the nutritional needs of your dog or cat.

Then make a habit of reading the labels on packages or cans of pet food.

And be sure to provide plenty of fresh water for your pet at all times.

Nutritional tips that dog owners should know

It's sometimes overlooked that dogs of different ages need different kinds of nutrition, according to Heinz's pet food division.

For instance, puppies need more calcium and phosphorus to accommodate their growing bodies. They also need more calories per pound than adult dogs and different amounts of certain vitamins and minerals.

Adult dog food, with more highly digestible grains and fat to provide proper energy, should be given after the pet reaches one year of age.

Senior and less-active dogs require fewer calories with managed levels of fat, especially for dogs who are putting on extra pounds. All dogs should get protein and essential amino acids to maintain muscles and keep the immune system strong. The proper amount and blend of Omega 6 and Omega 3 essential fatty acids are for a healthy shiny coat and healthy skin. Also needed for all dogs is balanced fiber for good regularity and a healthy gastrointestinal tract, along with the proper balance of vitamins and minerals.

The good news is that such dog food is available, by category, for pets of all ages.

Nutritional tips that cat owners should know

Cats require more protein and essential amino acids than dogs in order to keep their muscles, body systems and immune system working at peak efficiency.

That's why dog food should not be given to cats, and vice-versa.

Otherwise, the nutritional tips for dogs of different ages listed in the previous item also generally apply to cats—but pet owners should feed their cat the food that is especially made for kittens or adult felines.

By buying the proper food, pet owners can give cats and dogs good-tasting food that provides them with the right balance of nutrition needed for a healthy and happy life.

EIGHT

Amazing Advertising Facts

Eight

Amazing Advertising Facts

Advertisement that stretched the length of 3 football fields

Few people in the history of business ever went as far as Henry Heinz in promoting his company.

One of his incredible moves was to buy an ocean pier in Atlantic City, New Jersey—and this wasn't just a little pier. It extended the length of three football fields out into the Atlantic Ocean.

It was so big it contained a long boardwalk, a lounge, a reading room, a theater, a sun deck, exhibit hall, organ, and a glass pavilion with oriental rugs and works of art. On the roof was a 70-foot-high electric sign with a huge "57" that glowed at night and could be seen for miles.

Heinz bought the pier in 1898, and it was in use until destroyed by a hurricane in 1944.

It was free to the public and, of course, included displays of Heinz products, free pickle pins and free food samples.

Over the years, millions of people visited the Heinz Ocean Pier. And a popular postcard gave millions more a picture of the pier.

The pier was another example that helped Henry Heinz go down in history as a promotional genius.

What are the two most-recognized bottles in the world?

Coca-Cola and Heinz share the distinction of having created the most distinctive and recognizable bottles in history, according to many advertising experts.

Although Heinz started selling ketchup in 1876, it wasn't until 14 years later, or in 1890, that it developed the world-famous octagonal or eight-sided bottle.

The other all-time classic, Coca-Cola's distinctive, curved and fluted bottle, was created in the early 1900s.

The pickle pin is famous—but what about a ketchup pin?

While Heinz is known for pickles, it's even better known for ketchup; and yet there was no ketchup pin to match the popular pickle pin.

That changed on New Year's Day 2000, when Heinz introduced its new ketchup pin by giving 57,000 of them away around the world.

They were given to crowds in Paris, London, New Delhi, Beijing, Jakarta, Sydney, New Zealand, Hawaii, New York's Times Square, and at the Rose Bowl Parade in California.

Besides the 57,000 given away, Heinz stocked up with 1 million more. They are tomato red and shaped like the icon Heinz ketchup bottle, complete with a white keystone label, and will likely become valuable to collectors.

(To order, see page 218)

The "losing" commercial
that won big

One of the most famous TV commercials in history showed the sponsor losing—and yet, it was one of the most successful of all time.

Doyle Dane Bernbach, an advertising agency, created the commercial for Heinz showing a ketchup race between two bottles.

From one upside down bottle, the non-Heinz ketchup poured out quickly, like water. But from the Heinz bottle, the ketchup hardly moved; and the announcer said, "Heinz loses, Heinz always loses."

The message was that Heinz ketchup is "thick and rich," so it will always lose the "pouring" race.

But it proved a winner for Heinz because it established its uniqueness.

The only "57" product

Oddly enough, although Heinz uses "57" on their bottles and in advertising, only one product carries the company's famous "57" in its name.

That is its steak sauce, which is titled "Heinz 57 Sauce."

Advertising people are envious

People who work in advertising agencies, and specialists in the field, are often given the assignment to come up with slogans for companies.

Some they come up with are good, some are not. Few last very long.

So they have to be jealous of the businessman who was NOT an advertising professional, but who, on the spur of a moment, came up with a famous slogan that's lasted over 100 years.

In 1896, Henry Heinz created his "57 Varieties" slogan. And, by the way, he did it without any consultation, and without any market research or focus groups that many companies use today.

Old Henry himself probably would be surprised to learn that his slogan is STILL recognized, not only in the U.S., but around the world after all these years.

You can't win 'em all

In 1970, Heinz produced the most expensive television commercial ever made up to that time.

They hired famed and off-beat producer Stan Freeberg, who conceived and created a technically complex TV ad. It had a huge can of soup rising through the floor.

Movie star Ann Miller was employed to dance on top of the can, flanked by a large cast of other dancers.

The costly commercial was shot at the Samuel Goldwyn Studios in Hollywood and was as lavish as any TV ad could be.

The brand advertised was the new ready-to-serve product called the Great American Soup.

But despite the sensational commercial, and what was felt to be a good product, the Great American Soup brand never caught on with the public.

It was discontinued as a retail item.

Anticipation

Heinz loves to make commercials showing how thick their ketchup is and, therefore, how long it takes to come out of the bottle.

There was the famous "Heinz Loses" commercial—and in the early 1970s, their first memorable use of the song, *Anticipation,* written by Carly Simon. Heinz used the song to promote the slowness of their ketchup.

In 1990, their "Rooftop" commercial was voted Best of the Year. It showed an actor placing an open ketchup bottle on the edge of the roof of a five-story building. Then the actor ran down the five flights of stairs and rushed outside to have the ketchup slowly drip on the hot dog he was holding.

Heinz had trouble finding just the right actor to do the commercial. They finally found him.

Their choice: Matt LeBlanc who later would reach TV stardom in the hit sitcom, *Friends.*

The world without electric lights

It's hard to imagine now, but until the late 1800s, homes, offices, schools and streets had no electric lights.

Then Thomas Edison and others began to light the world with electricity—and the promotional genius, Henry Heinz, saw a new advertising opportunity. He could put his name in lights.

Heinz sponsored one of the first big electric signs in the world.

It was six stories high, on a building at 23rd Street and Fifth Avenue in New York City. It had a 43-foot-long pickle (with Heinz's name on it, of course) and 1,200 incandescent lights, advertising various Heinz messages.

Heinz had the sign erected in 1900; and it stayed up until the building was torn down to make way for the famous Flatiron Building.

Henry proved again that although he was a church-going, rather prudish man, he was never bashful about plastering his name and slogans wherever he could, in lights or otherwise.

What happened to the famous factory tours?

In the early days of the commercial food business, many manufacturers didn't want the public to see their factories. They were often dirty and unsanitary.

On the other hand, Henry Heinz always made a big thing about keeping his factory clean—both as a sense of pride and as a good public relations and advertising move. Thus, Heinz pioneered factory tours in 1899.

The Heinz plant tours, as they were called, became a major attraction in Pittsburgh for tourists and schoolchildren.

Millions of people made the tour over the years. There was a special staff of tour guides, and each visitor got a free pickle pin.

But after 73 years, in 1972, the tours ended. Why? Food processing had become so mechanized, there wasn't much to see. Where there used to be rows of women making ketchup, there were now machines doing the work.

What is a keystone?

There is no mystery why Heinz chose the shape of a keystone as the outline on many of its labels and in its advertising.

Heinz was founded in Pennsylvania, and Pennsylvania is known as "The Keystone State," because it was roughly in the middle of the original 13 U.S. states. A keystone is the KEY stone in the middle of an arch and holds the arch together. Early in Heinz history, they opted for the keystone.

If you've been married 57 years, you get a special gift

While silver says "Happy Anniversary" to couples wedded 25 years, and gold symbolizes 50th wedding anniversaries, there's a new way to say "Happy 57th."

A free gift of a crystal bell is offered by the Heinz company. The bell is etched with a big 57 on the Heinz keystone.

To receive this gift, anniversary couples send a copy of their marriage certificate and a letter signed by the wife and husband.

(See page 218 for address)

NINE

The Portrait of Pickles

Nine

The Portrait of Pickles

How pickles are made

A pickle is really a cured cucumber.

In a pickle factory, cucumbers are soaked in brine and flavored with seasonings such as dill, mustard, horseradish, cinnamon, vinegar, sugar, cloves, celery seed, peppercorn, and a mixture of spices.

The unique tastes of the various pickles—dill or spice or sweet—come about as the spices are added during the fermentation process when cucumbers are "pickled."

After the processing, pickles are either packaged whole or in slices.

The low-fat, low-calorie snack

If you're looking for a snack that has no fat and no calories, you might want to pick a pickle.

Genuine dill pickles have no fat or calories.

Sweet varieties of pickles do have some calories, but no fat.

Did you know
bees are responsible
for pickles?

While most people know bees are responsible for honey, few people realize the bee is also a vital part of pickles.

The common honeybee pollinates the blossoms in cucumber fields—and, of course, the cucumber is the basis for a pickle.

If a cucumber blossom is not pollinated, the cucumber drops from its vine prematurely and can not be harvested.

To ensure the pollination of cucumbers, Heinz and its growers rent hundreds of beehives each season. One hive, which has between 20,000 and 90,000 bees, pollinates one acre of growing cucumbers.

The rent-a-bee project helps Heinz increase its cucumber crop by 50 percent.

This is no small delivery

How would you like to open your door in the morning and find 25,000 bushels of cucumbers being delivered to you.

That's what happens EVERY DAY during the May-September season at the Heinz pickle factory in Holland, Michigan.

That factory has 500 tanks that brine, or marinate in salt-saturated water, more than 700,000 bushels of pickles a year from those cucumbers.

The most popular variety of pickle is the kosher dill, but they also make more than 25 other varieties.

Why do we say a person is "in a pickle"?

"How camest thou in such a pickle" is a quote from "The Tempest," written by William Shakespeare more than 400 years ago. Since then, pickles and predicaments have been synonymous.

Pickle fun facts

- The world's largest pickle factory is in Holland, Michigan. The Heinz pickle factory there includes 17 buildings, with a total of 500,000 square feet covering 28 acres. More than 200 varieties of pickles, peppers, relishes and vinegar are made at that facility.
- Almost two-thirds of Americans buy pickles each year. Americans eat more than 29 BILLION pickles annually.
- The most preferred flavor of pickles is kosher dill.
- North Americans like pickles with "warts" or bumps. Europeans generally prefer wartless pickles.
- Pickle flavors include dill, Kosher dill, Polish dill, sweet and gherkin. Kosher, in regard to pickles, means the pickles are garlic-flavored. Polish dill means some garlic and spices. Gherkins come from a small, whole cucumber and can have either a sweet or sour flavor.
- Singer Bing Crosby's first job was selling pickles.

TEN

Around the World

Surprisingly, spaghetti didn't originate in Italy

The name "spaghetti" comes from Italian, where it literally means "little strings," but spaghetti itself was first made a long way from Italy.

It was the Chinese who invented spaghetti more than 3,000 years ago.

Legend has it that the Italian, Marco Polo, brought spaghetti to Italy from his famous China trip in the 13th century.

For many years after that, it did not become popular throughout the world. Making spaghetti was a laborious process. The noodles had to be rolled and cut by hand, and then the long strings were hung out to dry in the sun.

It wasn't until the 1920s that spaghetti began to reach a world market with modern bottling, canning and packaging. Interestingly, Heinz sells canned spaghetti and pasta around the world, but not in the U.S.

How popular are baked beans in England?

It's no secret that people who live on the British Isles like baked beans. They are, by far, one of the most popular foods there—but the recent results of a survey show just how popular.

Heinz asked 1,000 people what they would miss most if they left the U.K. Amazingly, almost half the respondents said baked beans.

Based on that, Heinz U.K. launched a Web site, www.heinz-direct.co.uk, where consumers around the world, including British expatriates, can order their beloved baked beans.

Patriotism costs Heinz

To help the war effort during World War II, Heinz converted their baby food factory in Pittsburgh to making gliders for the military.

By stopping the making of baby food for four years during the war, Heinz gave Gerber a virtual monopoly. When Heinz reentered the baby food market after the war, they never got their market share back in the U.S., although they do lead in baby food in Canada, the U.K., Australia and Italy.

Misspelling
creates hit

Heinz purposely allowed the word "beans" to be misspelled in an advertisement—and it became one of the most successful ads of all time.

In Britain, Heinz ran a campaign for its baked beans in the 1970s and employed the Young & Rubicam ad agency.

The agency came up with "Beanz Meanz Heinz." It became a classic line and a national catch-phrase—with many variations dreamed up by the public (some printable, some not).

Heinz used its own variations, such as showing children smiling while eating beans under the heading of "Heinz Beamz."

The ad campaign helped solidify the connection between beans and Heinz and kept Heinz No. 1 in the market.

They misspelled another word-- and got success again

Not to let a good thing die after the "Beanz Meanz Heinz" success, Heinz turned attention to its soups in Britain.

They played around with many phrases, changing the spelling of "super" to "soup," as in "Heinz Souper Day," "Souper Year," "Heinz Souperman" and "Souper Savings."

Heinz again had created a memorable campaign and strengthened their market share in soups.

Latest figures show Heinz sells nearly one million cans of soup a day in Britain.

That's a lot of beans

Although baked beans are popular in many countries of the world, nobody eats them like the British.

An almost unbelievable number of baked beans are sold in Britain. Heinz says the British market consumes 1.5 million cans of baked beans EVERY DAY.

Beans on Toast

Heinz executive Charles Hellen was sent from the Pittsburgh headquarters to its British company in 1927 and came up with an idea.

Thinking about ways to sell more baked beans, Hellen created a national dish—BEANS ON TOAST, introducing the idea of having beans for breakfast as well as dinner.

Today, eating beans on toast is a tradition in the British Isles.

Hellen, ahead of his time...

By emphasizing the health benefits of beans, Hellen was ahead of his time as he advertised that beans are low-fat, high-fiber and "build body, brain and muscle."

During the Great Depression years of the 1930s, he promoted beans' high nutrition and said, "Every pound of Heinz Baked Beans is equal in value to one pound of prime steak—at a lower cost."

Baked beans became a national habit in Britain, and they still are.

They make "Kecap"

In Indonesia, a popular product is a sauce called "kecap," which is consumed with virtually every meal as either a table-top condiment or ingredient.

Although that's close to the word "ketchup" in the area of the world where ketchup originated, kecap is not ketchup. Kecap is a sweet soy sauce.

It's made by the ABC company, which is now part of Heinz. Heinz bought the controlling interest in ABC in 1999 in a venture called PT Heinz ABC Indonesia—so they now sell both ABC kecap and Heinz ketchup throughout Southeast Asia.

It's an interesting East-West marriage of the world's leading ketchup brand with the world's second-largest producer of soy sauces.

ABC also makes "kecap asin," which is a salty soy sauce and "sambal," a hot chili sauce.

Food companies love China

More people on earth live in China than any other country. China has almost 25 percent of the world's population.

That's a lot of mouths to feed; but for many years, western companies couldn't supply food there.

That began to change in 1984 when the People's Republic of China invited Heinz to produce dry infant cereal.

With more than 20 million babies born in China each year, Heinz eagerly entered into a joint venture to bring its baby food to this huge market.

Heinz has expanded its presence there with more baby food products, such as reciped jarred baby foods and ketchup.

O Canada

Although Canada and the U.S. are next-door neighbors, the taste preference in ketchup is different in the two countries.

When a U.S. resident visits Canada, he or she finds Heinz ketchup there is not quite the same as in the States.

Canadians prefer a sweeter ketchup. Heinz, which adapts its food for local tastes around the world, manufactures its ketchup specifically for Canadians in Canadian factories.

Heinz came to Canada in 1909. Heinz products are so big there that some Canadians, like the British, feel that Heinz is their company with a U.S. subsidiary.

Besides being No. 1 in ketchup in Canada, Heinz also leads all other Canadian brands in baby food and is one of the top pet food suppliers.

The biggest contest ever

In the history of business, no company ever ran a contest like Heinz did.

To celebrate their 100th year in Britain, in 1986, Heinz gave away 100 automobiles—one day at a time—customized with the nameplate "H57."

How big was this promotion?

There are only about 60 million people living in the United Kingdom, which translates into about 19 million households. More than one out of every two households in the entire nation responded to the promotion. Heinz received over 11 million entries, an incredible response.

And, incredible publicity for the company.

What's
a Wattie?

The big name in food products in New Zealand and elsewhere in the Pacific Rim is Wattie's.

Now a Heinz company, Wattie's was founded in 1934 in a four-room cottage in the small town of Hastings, New Zealand, by two accountants—James Wattie and Henry Carr.

They sold shares to 28 local people, and James Wattie became the managing director.

The company grew to such an influence in the food industry that James Wattie was later knighted and became known as Sir James Wattie.

Today, Wattie's makes everything from frozen vegetables to fresh and frozen chicken, to animal feeds to baby foods, plus many canned goods.

When Heinz bought Wattie's in 1992, it was Heinz's biggest-ever overseas acquisition.

Whoever heard
of trademarking
a color?

Usually trademarks in the business world are given to names or logos, but there's been an unusual trademark granted in the United Kingdom.

The turquoise color used on cans of Heinz Baked Beans in the U.K. was trademarked by a government agency—because that color on beans has become such a big part of the culture.

A Heinz executive says, "Our baked beans have been the number-one brand for generations, and the Trademarks Registry is quite right to grant this trademark."

That's odd because, with other products everywhere, nothing stops competitors from using red cans or blue cans or whatever; but in the U.K., competitors are deterred from putting their baked beans in a turquoise can.

The different ways
the world uses
ketchup

Americans are used to ketchup on hamburgers, hot dogs and french fries—but in other countries, ketchup is used on so many different foods.

In Britain, it's used on fish and chips.

The Chinese like to use it on fried chicken.

Both the Spaniards and people in India like ketchup atop omelets and other egg dishes served at breakfast, lunch and dinner.

Swedes favor the flavor of ketchup on pasta.

Teens in Thailand dip potato chips in ketchup.

In eastern Europe, ketchup is a favorite topping for pizza.

And, many Asians use ketchup on seafood, especially shrimp, when stir-fried or deep-fried.

Ketchup goes "home"
with a new body

As mentioned before, ketchup originated in China, long before Western nations had it.

Now ketchup is coming back to its homeland—but this is a different ketchup.

When the Chinese originally made it, they used pickled fish as the main ingredient, instead of tomatoes.

But now, Heinz has made a deal to make and sell its tomato ketchup in China as that country emerges as one of the economic powers of the new century.

The odyssey of ketchup has thus made a complete round trip, picking up new ingredients on its long journey as the world's favorite condiment.

ELEVEN

How Safe Is Your Food?

Eleven

How Safe Is Your Food?

Thousands die from unsafe food

One-hundred years ago, there were few laws protecting people from unsanitary conditions found sometimes in producing food sold to consumers.

No one knows how many people got sick or died because of the lack of sanitation and the use of harmful ingredients by unscrupulous manufacturers.

Today's experts estimate that it must have been untold thousands.

Three major events turned things around. One was a book by Upton Sinclair, "The Jungle," published in 1906, which exposed the filthy conditions in the meat-packing industry.

About this same time, the science of microbiology came into being. Microbiologists were able to detect unwanted bacteria and unsafe additives in food processing.

And, finally, the U.S. government adopted the first pure food laws in the early 1900s, but it took a while to take full effect. It wasn't until around 1915 that virtually all food sold in stores was safe.

"It's none of your business"

A food company employee tells the story about the customer who wrote to a manufacturer, asking what ingredients were in a package of food she had just bought.

This was in the days before companies were required to list ingredients on their packages.

The manufacturer directed that the customer be told, "It's none of your damn business what we put in our food."

Such philosophy was not unusual when some food processors wanted to keep their ingredients secret, either for competitive reasons or unscrupulous ones, or both.

Today, such secrets are uncommon in many countries of the world.

Those nutritional guidelines on food are a relatively recent development

Surprisingly, there was no federal law in the United States requiring nutritional facts to be listed on food products until 1990.

Now you'll find daily values for nutrients on food labels. The Nutrition Facts panel allows you to read and compare nutritional information and to understand its relative significance in the context of your daily diet.

The law mandates the size of the nutrition panel and where it's placed on every label.

The Nutrition Facts must give you information on such things as calories, fat, cholesterol, protein, potassium, sodium, carbohydrate, vitamins and percent of daily values.

Smart shoppers should take advantage of labels by reading and comparing them.

Henry Heinz's religious zeal had role in today's food rules

From all historical accounts, Heinz founder Henry Heinz was a very religious man in both his personal and business life.

Although he was an aggressive businessman, he always seemed to preach—and practice—high moral standards.

He constantly spoke and wrote about using only the best ingredients and pioneered principles that affected the then-new commercial food industry.

The proof was his action in 1906 when the government was trying to pass the Pure Food and Drug Act.

At that time, without government regulation, some manufacturers turned out terrible—and sometimes lethal—food. They added harmful chemicals to improve flavor and color. Their factories were filthy. Mislabeling and false advertising were common.

Henry stood virtually alone within the industry in advocating food laws. Even some people in the general public were against legislation which they saw as government intervention in personal liberty.

Heinz's competitors spread rumors about him, and he was seen as a traitor within his own industry. It was a vicious fight.

Actually, Henry thought it was not only a moral issue—but it was good business to enact food safety laws. He felt the industry would grow if consumers had more confidence in the food they were buying.

After much lobbying by Heinz and public interest groups, Congressional hearings were held. Medical men testified to Congress on the effects of harmful ingredients.

On June 23, 1906, Congress passed the landmark Pure Food and Drug Act. That day marked the beginning of the modern food industry. With the law, people began buying more food products. The industry prospered—and so did Heinz.

How bad whiskey led to good food

When Henry Heinz was campaigning for passage of pure food and drug legislation, he sent his son Howard and a chemist to lobby President Theodore Roosevelt.

Roosevelt, at the time, was not convinced the law was necessary. The chemist, Dr. Harvey Wiley of the Department of Agriculture, tried to convince the President. But Roosevelt remained skeptical until Wiley took out a bottle of whiskey.

Wiley adulterated the whiskey and gave Roosevelt a drink. It was terrible. Roosevelt said, "If a man can't get a good drink of whiskey when he comes home from work, then there ought to be a law to see that he does."

Teddy Roosevelt joined the fight and lobbied Congress to pass the Pure Food and Drug Act.

There's some irony to this story. Henry Heinz reportedly never drank or smoked in his life, but a shot of whiskey gave a shot in the arm to his campaign for the Pure Food Act.

In what order are ingredients listed on food packages and bottles?

There's a specific order to the list of ingredients you see on packages and bottles of food.

Listed first is what there is the most of. Other ingredients are listed in descending order of quantity.

For example, on the Heinz 57 Sauce label, tomato paste is listed first, which means there's more of that than anything else. Then all the other ingredients are listed in order of quantity used.

TWELVE

The Hitch

Twelve

The Hitch

Why Heinz
uses the Hitch

Millions of people have seen the Heinz Hitch, which is a wagon drawn by eight black Percheron horses.

The Hitch performs at fairs, parades and expositions across North America every year—and in such events as New York's Macy's Thanksgiving Day Parade, Pasadena's Tournament of Roses Parade and many festivals.

The reason Heinz created the Hitch is for a living history lesson. In the days before trucks, Heinz used more than 100 Percheron horse-drawn wagons to deliver their products to stores—and the current Hitch is reminiscent of the ones used by H.J. Heinz himself in the early days of the company.

How the original Hitch was found

The 130-year-old current Heinz Hitch was abandoned for 50 years and then was discovered in a storage shed in central Pennsylvania in 1978.

The old wood was restored and painted along with all the original metal framing and connecting pieces.

Today's Hitch wagon weighs 6,800 pounds and is said to be the world's largest now in use.

To pull that 6,800-pound wagon, Heinz uses the eight Percheron horses, who weigh more than one ton each and generate 16,000 pounds of horsepower.

Stars in their own right

Today's Percherons, used with the Hitch, give audiences a memorable show. Besides pulling the 6,800-pound Hitch, they perform a demonstration of equestrian obedience and crowd-pleasing maneuvers.

One maneuver is called "Fanning" as they swing 180° without moving the wagon. In "Spin the Top," the Percherons make a circle while the inside Hitch wheel stays in place.

Getting there from here

One of the most-often asked questions regarding the Heinz Hitch is how those eight big horses get from one place to another for their more than 100 appearances across North America each year.

They travel about 57,000 miles a year on highways going from city to city in a new, first-class (for horses) trailer. It's not air conditioned because horses can get sick if they're moved quickly from air conditioning to a hot summer day outside. However, the trailer has individual fans for each horse that keeps the air moving inside.

The 50-foot-long horse trailer usually takes 10 Percherons on trips—the eight who perform, plus two in reserve in case of injury or illness to any of the eight first-stringers.

The motorcade that moves the Hitch around the country consists of four trucks and trailers for the Hitch, the horses, the crew and supplies.

Also in the group are the two Dalmatians who ride on top of the Hitch—Barbie (short for barbecue sauce) and H.J., named for the Heinz founder. The dogs are very protective of the horses, sleeping near them every night, ready to bark an alarm if there's any danger.

Why they're called "Percheron" horses

Percheron horses got their name from the Perche region of France, where they were bred specifically to blend power, speed and agility.

Those attributes made Percherons a favored horse during the time when armored knights rode into battle. The horses wore heavy armor, too.

Knights wanted a big, powerful horse that would stand up in a battle and would be harder to bring down. Because if the horse was killed, the horseless knight was defenseless. Knights also wanted a horse that had speed and maneuverability.

Percherons chosen for color and cobblestone

Henry Heinz had two reasons for choosing Percherons to pull his delivery wagons back in the 1800s.

He liked their black color, which presented a good contrast with his red wagons. Henry felt it was good advertising for people to see the familiar Heinz red wagons and black horses coming down the street.

Then too, the Percherons were perfect for negotiating the hills in the Pittsburgh area where Heinz started, and the tough cobblestone streets that were common then.

How many people see the Hitch?

It's estimated that more than six million people see the Hitch perform every year.

That's in addition to TV viewers of the annual Pasadena Tournament of Roses Parade which is televised to more than 100 countries. Interestingly, at the Rose Parade, the Hitch is placed 57th in line, honoring Heinz's "57 Varieties" slogan.

Those wanting to have the Hitch at a future event, see page 218.

THIRTEEN

The Head Men at Heinz

Thirteen

The Head Men at Heinz

Only six CEOs
in 131 years

Amazingly, in its first 131 years, Heinz has had just six chief executives.

The company was founded when Ulysses Grant was U.S. President, in 1869. There have been 25 Presidents of the United States from 1869 to 2000, but in that time, only six heads of Heinz.

The six include three family members and three who were non-family.

Henry, Howard and Jack Heinz led Heinz from 1869 into the 1960s.

After almost 100 years of only someone named Heinz heading the company, Burt Gookin was appointed CEO in 1966.

Gookin was followed by Tony O'Reilly in 1979. Bill Johnson took over from O'Reilly as President-CEO in 1998, and O'Reilly remained as Chairman until 2000.

The odd habit
of Howard Heinz

When Howard Heinz took over from his father, Henry, as head of Heinz in 1919, he developed the habit of sharing financial information with no one in the company.

Howard, alone, would get the figures from all his divisions.

Then, this CEO of a giant, global company would sit at his desk and add up all the numbers on backs of envelopes. Howard, reportedly, didn't even use an adding machine; and, of course, there were no computers.

According to company legend, when Howard's treasurer would show him a piece of paper with a particular financial figure on it, Howard would note it and then have the treasurer tear it up.

Heinz had no obligation to report earnings publicly then because it was still a private company, but Howard also kept the information secret even from his top managers.

During his reign, Howard, himself, thus, made all the key decisions on pricing, research, new products and advertising.

Howard convinces father
that college men are okay

Henry Heinz built a great company without any business degree. In fact, Henry never attended college at all, which was not unusual for successful people in his day.

But his son, Howard, was Yale-educated, majored in chemistry and studied nutrition.

Howard had to fight his father's distrust of college men, scientists and chemists. He was able, finally, to convince his father to hire bacteriologists and adapt scientific methods in processing, preservation and production of foods.

Before that, although Henry led the national fight for safe food, the methods used to achieve it were mostly seat-of-the-pants and unscientific.

Howard's other contributions to the growth of Heinz came during his tenure as CEO, when he added baby foods and soups, and guided the company successfully through the Great Depression.

Personally, according to company historians, Howard was most proud of the fact that he never laid off a salaried worker during the Depression.

33-year-old man
heads Heinz

Jack Heinz became one of the youngest men to head a major global corporation.

He took over as CEO of Heinz when his father, Howard, died unexpectedly at age 64 in 1941.

At the beginning of his reign, the 33-year-old Jack operated much like his father. Jack involved himself in decisions that "someone like him shouldn't have," according to a former employee—such as picking baby food labels and deciding whether a particular recipe tasted right.

In many ways, both Howard and Jack ran Heinz like a sole proprietorship, and not a worldwide corporation.

That began to change in 1946 when Heinz made the first public stock offering in its 77-year history.

The days of keeping profits and losses secret were over.

Jack's
crown jewels

Before Jack Heinz became CEO in 1941, the Heinz company never acquired another company. His grandfather, Henry, and farther, Howard, built the company with internal growth.

But during Jack's tenure, he broke with tradition and oversaw the purchase of StarKist and Ore-Ida, bringing them into the Heinz family—giving the company two of their leading brands today.

Jack also had another shining moment that was both humanitarian and good public relations. In 1947, he led a national campaign to feed the hungry children of post-war Europe.

He donated one million packages of baby food and pledged in national ads to donate "another package for every package of baby food bought by mothers throughout the United States" during one week of April.

Almost five million food packages were distributed.

The sports connection

Burt Gookin was the first non-Heinz to become CEO of the Heinz company, and he began a string of three consecutive CEOs with a sports connection.

Gookin's father had been a pro baseball player who cut down a regular-sized set of golf clubs for Burt to use when he was six years old.

By the time he was 13, Burt won a club championship and grew up to be an avid, accomplished amateur golfer.

He was also a Golden Gloves boxer in his youth and went to Northwestern University on a scholarship, making both the golf and boxing teams.

Golf helped Gookin get his MBA. While working for Firestone after his undergraduate days, he won club championships at the Firestone Country Club. That caught the eye of some Firestone Harvard Business School alumns who helped Burt get a Harvard scholarship.

Gookin joined Heinz in 1945 and rose to CEO in 1966. During his tenure as head of Heinz from then until 1979, he increased sales three-fold.

He also brought professional management techniques to the former family-run business.

How many major companies have been headed by a world-class athlete?

Before Tony O'Reilly succeeded Burt Gookin as head of Heinz in 1979, O'Reilly was an international sports star.

O'Reilly grew up in Ireland and became a world-class rugby player at age 19.

He was the youngest member of the championship British Lions all-star team, representing the best players from England, Scotland, Ireland and Wales.

On tour with the Lions to South Africa in 1955, he set records for try-scoring (similar to touchdowns in American football) with 16.

In 1959, the Lions toured Australasia; and in New Zealand, O'Reilly scored 17.

Those became all-time world records.

The unusual O'Reilly

By the time he was 33 years old, Tony O'Reilly had not only been a rugby star, but an honor student in college and law school and a successful businessman in Ireland and England.

Among other things, he had created an international food brand—Kerrygold dairy products, which became Ireland's biggest export organization, with sales of about $2 billion.

He joined Heinz at age 33 as a manager of an off-shore affiliate and, in just 10 years, had a meteoric rise to CEO of the entire Heinz company.

During his CEO tenure, O'Reilly launched Heinz into a new era in which the company became a leader in the nutrition and wellness revolution and its expansion into more countries—especially those in the emerging markets of Asia, sending Heinz to new heights.

NFL head coach's son
heads multinational corporation

From 1976 until 1978, the head coach of the Cincinnati Bengals of the National Football League was Bill "Tiger" Johnson.

Johnson had succeeded the Hall of Fame coaching legend, Paul Brown, as Bengals coach.

Johnson won 18 games over all and lost 15, but resigned part way through the 1978 season.

His son, William R. Johnson, took a different career path, and rose to become president and chief executive officer of the H.J. Heinz Company in 1998.

How Johnson rose to the
the head of Heinz

It wasn't football, like his dad had played and coached, but the younger Bill Johnson entered the competitive world of consumer products.

He managed brands for Drackett, Ralston Purina, Frito Lay and Anderson Clayton before joining Heinz in 1982.

Johnson did keep his hand in football along

the way, working in marketing for the pro football Hall of Fame in Canton, Ohio.

At Heinz, Johnson became head of pet food products in 1988, doubling sales and quadrupling profits.

In 1992, Johnson was put in charge of StarKist and increased their share of the market. A year later, his duties expanded to Heinz operations in the Asia-Pacific area.

Johnson was named president and CEO of the Heinz company in 1998.

He's a graduate of UCLA and got his MBA from the University of Texas.

FOURTEEN

Pot-Pourri

Fourteen

Pot-Pourri

What are the 2 most popular items at grocery stores?

According to the company that tracks total purchases at supermarkets and grocery stores in the U.S., the most popular item is Coca Cola Classic® in two-liter bottles. The second-most popular item is StarKist tuna.

Where football tailgating began

One of America's favorite customs is tailgating at football games where popular food products and football meet.

Historians say the custom started on the extensive lawns surrounding the Yale Bowl in New Haven, Connecticut in the 1920s. Yale grads drove up to New Haven from the New York City area and enjoyed a lunch around their cars before going into the stadium to see that day's football game.

Interestingly, American college football and the Heinz company both started in the same year, 1869.

How tomatoes were proved to be not poisonous

Very few people ate tomatoes until the 1800s because of the fear they were poisonous.

Col. Robert G. Johnson wanted to dispel that myth.

During an historic moment in Salem, New Jersey, he did something dramatic to change the history of food.

At a public demonstration on Sept. 26, 1830, he walked to the steps of the courthouse in Salem. He took a bite out of a tomato, and then another and another.

Nothing happened to him.

He said he always felt tomatoes were not poisonous—and he proved it.

Salem, New Jersey, became a big tomato-growing area after that, and tomatoes became a major food everywhere.

What does that "U" in a circle stand for?

If you've ever noticed that some food products you buy have a small circle with the letter "U" on their labels, here's what that symbol means.

The food inside is kosher or suitable to eat for those who adhere to kosher diets.

The "U" stands for the Union of Orthodox Jewish Congregations, and it is their kosher seal of approval. Only products endorsed by that Union are permitted to carry the seal. The letter "O," represented by the circle, stands for "orthodox."

The first kosher-approved national products were Heinz's, in 1923.

The "Circle U" first appeared on Heinz vegetarian beans that year.

To earn the seal, factory procedures have to be inspected by rabbis to make sure strict start-up and cleanup rules are followed.

Today, nearly 80,000 products in 48 countries use the "Circle U."

Old bottles lost—then found

Few American companies have been in business as long as Heinz—but a sentimental part of their history was almost wiped out.

Heinz always saved old labels, bottles, cans, advertisements and other artifacts going back to 1869. They were preserved in one of their factory buildings along the Allegheny River in Pittsburgh.

However, a devastating flood destroyed everything there in 1936, and Heinz was left without these pieces of history.

Amazingly, it turns out that people everywhere had saved and collected old Heinz artifacts. Ed Lehew, former Heinz advertising executive, says people call all the time, offering Heinz memorabilia. Lehew, himself, visits antique shops and flea markets looking for items.

One day, a woman called Lehew to say she found an old ketchup bottle in her basement. She brought it in, and it turned out to be a real prize. It was from 1876, the first year Heinz made ketchup—with ketchup then spelled "catsup" on the bottle. "Incredibly," says Lehew, "the bottle was in perfect condition."

Today, Heinz memorabilia ranks among the most popular company collectibles in the world.

Boston Market goes to the freezer

Boston Market has licensed their trademark to Heinz for the manufacture and sale of frozen grocery food products.

Under the name of Boston Market Home Style Meals®, Heinz makes a menu of full meals, individual meat items and side dishes, allowing shoppers to create their own meals.

Why is it called Boston Market?

The Boston Market® restaurant chain has had their headquarters a long way from Boston. Their main offices have been in Naperville, Illinois and Golden, Colorado—and the factories that make the Boston Market line of food for Heinz are in Massillon, Ohio, and Pocatello, Idaho.

So why is it "Boston" Market? They started with a single restaurant in 1985 called "Boston Chicken" in a Boston, Massachusetts suburb.

But they soon moved their headquarters to Naperville and then Golden, keeping their Boston name. In 1995, they switched from "Boston Chicken" to "Boston Market."

Celebrity's name
on food

One of the popular products in Great Britain are the Linda McCartney vegetarian/meat-free foods.

They carry the name of the late wife of Paul McCartney of Beatles fame—but this is no celebrity-testimonial use of a famous name.

During her lifetime, Linda McCartney was an ardent animal rights advocate and a vegetarian herself. She was instrumental in starting the successful food company that bears her name.

Her husband, now known as Sir Paul McCartney (also a vegetarian), continued the company after her death.

Heinz recently purchased the Linda McCartney brand, which is sold throughout Britain.

A popular Linda McCartney product is sausages. The meat-free version of the "Great British Banger" is big with vegetarians and meat eaters.

Other popular products are Deep County Pies, Flamed Grilled Burgers (no meat, of course), Easy Cook Mince and lasagna.

Watching weight

Weight Watchers was started by a 40-year-old, overweight New York woman, Jean Nidetch, in 1962.

Jean lost the weight she wanted through a weight-loss regimen she got from the New York City Department of Health, and she later joined Al and Felice Lippert in forming a worldwide company called Weight Watchers International.

The Lipperts were instrumental in adding a line of foods to the Weight Watchers classrooms and sold the company to Heinz for $100 million in 1978.

Heinz then developed a whole array of Weight Watchers foods—working at making low-calorie food taste better.

One of the first big hits was a low-calorie dessert of chocolate mousse.

Then in 1999, Heinz sold off the Weight Watchers classroom part of the company—but kept the foods, such as Smart Ones from Weight Watchers, which include frozen meals, desserts and breakfast items in the U.S. Around the world, Heinz also sells Weight Watchers Food.

From one woman determined to lose weight, Weight Watchers developed into one of the most successful weight-control businesses.

Why people live longer today

It's hard to believe now, but average life expectancy at birth in the U.S. in 1900 was just 49 years of age. Today, average life expectancy has increased to more than 70 years of age. That's an incredibly dramatic gain in human life spans.

There are many sociological and medical reasons for the increase, but one of the main factors centers on more healthful eating.

Babies didn't have baby food

Years ago, there was no commercial food made especially for babies. In fact, very little was known about nutrition then.

But as the 20th century unfolded, companies began making baby food—as both a convenience to parents, and a new source of nutritious food for babies.

The revolution in longer life spans continues, starting with kids growing up to be bigger and healthier, in part due to better nutrition in infant years.

Incredible giant feeds infants

In the history of making food safe, nothing ever approached an amazing giant of a machine that was made to sterilize baby food.

Called a Hydrostatic Sterilizer, this machine stood seven stories high and weighed more than 250 tons.

It could sterilize the unbelievable total of 180,000 jars of baby food at one time.

The machine, the first of its kind in the world, was developed by Heinz in 1974 and was recently replaced by its second-generation cousin.

After some 180,000 jars of baby food are fed into this gigantic piece of equipment, it uses super heat to sterilize the product. The machine has dozens of pumps, valves and instrument-sensing ports all controlling the process into a central computer.

After two-and-half hours, the jars come out ready for labeling.

This machine, located in Pittsburgh, runs 24 hours a day for five or six days a week depending on demand, and it produces virtually all the baby food sold by Heinz in the U.S., as well as export markets throughout the world.

Heinz's failures

Along with their thousands of popular products, Heinz has had some spectacular failures.

They made Superman® hot cocoa and thought it would be a big hit because of the name. But the kids it was intended for didn't like it.

They got the idea of putting edible sparkles in ketchup, figuring kids would like that—but they didn't.

Millions were spent on producing an instant baby food. Mothers could add more or less water to give their babies differing thicknesses of food. It sounded good, but moms didn't like it because it was more bother than ready-to-eat baby food.

Happy Soup, heavily advertised with Disney characters, had a brief flurry of success but then failed.

And Heinz promoted a Senior Foods brand— but found that seniors didn't want to be seen buying a product with that name.

The incredible similarities
over 3 centuries

The fascinating story of Heinz is the amazing connection of 19th-20th-and-21st-century customs coming together.

Consumers in the 1800s bought Heinz ketchup, vinegar and pickles. So did consumers in the 1900s, and so they do in the 2000s.

But it's not just the products. Henry Heinz gave away popular pickle pins in the 1800s. In 2000, his company took the same idea and began giving away ketchup pins.

Henry used a hitch and horses to make deliveries in the 1800s, and today one of his original hitches is still used to entertain 21st century audiences.

Take a walk through the Heinz factory site in Pittsburgh today, and you'll be on the same spot where Heinz products were made in the 1800s.

Despite creating so much history, Henry, himself, was a futurist. He pioneered concepts of worldwide distribution, adding new products at a rapid rate, advocating safe food rules, and capitalizing on the then-new practices of public relations and promotions.

FIFTEEN

International Recipes

FUN RECIPES USING HEINZ PRODUCTS

These international recipes are courtesy of the H. J. Heinz Company and the two authors. **ALL RECIPES ARE LISTED BY COUNTRY.**

Remember, Heinz products vary in flavor, texture, and consistency from one country to another. Often, the results will differ when using one country's ketchup in another country's recipe. That's not to say it won't be good; it just might taste differently than the original recipe-giver intended.

Following is a chart for help in conversions from "The Cook's Book of Essential Information" by Barbara Hill.

If the recipe calls for	Multiply by	To find
teaspoons	5	milliliters
tablespoons	15	milliliters
fluid ounces	30	milliliters
cups	0.24	liters
pints	0.47	liters
quarts	0.94	liters
ounces (by weight)	28	grams
pounds	0.45	kilograms

"A rule of thumb is that a kilogram is 'a little more' than 2 pounds. For ease of figuring, it is probably more convenient to round the conversions off, for instance, figuring an ounce to be equivalent to about 25 grams."

Or for those of us who don't like math, the following conversion chart might be helpful.

ING HEINZ TOMATO KETCHUP IN U.S.

T FOOTBALL FRANKS

p Heinz Tomato Ketchup
n (8 oz.) crushed pineapple in juice, undrained
cup grape jelly
2 tbsp. chopped jalapeño peppers
cocktail franks

bine ketchup, pineapple, jelly and jalapeños.
k over medium heat until jelly is melted. Stir in
ks; and heat. Serve warm with picks. Makes 12-
ervings.

¼ tsp (teaspoon)	1 ml
½ tsp (teaspoon)	3 ml
1 tsp (teaspoon)	5 ml
1 T (tablespoon)	1 tablespoon
¼ cup=2 tablespoons=2 fluid ounces=60 ml	
1/3 C (cup)=4 fluid ounces	120 ml
½ C (cup)	125 ml
½ C (cup)=5 fluid ounces	150 ml
¾ C (cup)	175 ml
¾ C (cup)=6 fluid oz.	180 ml.
1 C (cup)	250 ml
1 C (cup)=8 fluid ounces	240ml.
12 oz. (ounces)	340 g
½ lb (pound)	225 g
1 lb (pound)	450 g
1 quart	1 L

Barbara Hill again, "In cooking absolute precision is, fortunately, not required or even desired…a good approximation will do very nicely."

Some common American ingredients and their possible counterparts:
- Powdered sugar is icing sugar.
- Sugar is granulated or castor sugar.
- Light corn syrup is golden syrup.
- Cornstarch is cornflour.

- All-purpose flour is plain household flour or white flour. When self-rising flour is used in place of all-purpose flour in a recipe that calls for leavening, omit the leavening agent (baking soda or baking powder) and salt.
- Baking soda is bicarbonate of soda.
- Vanilla is vanilla essence.
- Green, red, or yellow bell peppers are capsicums.
- Golden raisins are sultanas.

Volume and Weight
- 1 cup butter, castor sugar or rice=8 oz.= about 250 grams
- 1 cup flour=4 oz.= about 125 grams
- 1 cup icing sugar=5 oz. =about 150 grams

Oven Temperatures

Fahrenheit Setting	Celsius Setting	Gas Mark
300F°	150C°	2 (slow)
325F°	160C°	3 (moderately slow)
350F°	180C°	4 (moderate)
375F°	190C°	5 (moderately hot)
400F°	200C°	6 (hot)
425F°	220C°	7
450F°	230C°	8 (very hot)
Broil		Grill

For electric oven, increase the Celsius setting 10 to 20 degrees when cooking above 160°C.

USING HEINZ TOMATO K
IN U.S.

US

PARMESAN PASTA AND VEGETAF

FA

8 ounces uncooked penne pasta
1 can (15 ½ oz.) Italian-style diced tomato
1 bag (16 oz.) frozen Italian-style vegetabl
1/2 cup Heinz Tomato Ketchup
1/3 cup water
1/2 teaspoon dried oregano leaves
1/4 cup grated Parmesan cheese

1 c
1 c
1/2
1 t
1 t

Cook penne according to package direction
warm. Meanwhile, in large skillet, combine
tomatoes, vegetables, ketchup, water and or
Cover; cook 6 to 7 minutes or until vegetab
tender-crisp. Stir in pasta and Parmesan. H
Serve with additional Parmesan cheese, if d
Makes 4 servings (about 7 cups).

Cc
Cc
fra
15

KETCHUP 'N HONEY DUNK

1 cup Heinz Tomato Ketchup
1/4 cup honey

Mix ingredients together. Serve with chic
nuggets.

USING HEINZ TOMATO KETCHUP IN U.S.

BOWLING NIGHT CHILI

2 medium onions, chopped
1 green bell pepper, chopped
2 tablespoons vegetable oil
2 pounds lean ground beef or turkey
2 to 3 tablespoons chili powder
1 can (14 ½ oz.) diced tomatoes
1 can (15 oz.) tomato sauce
1/2 cup Heinz Tomato Ketchup
1 teaspoon salt
1/2 teaspoon pepper
2 cans (15 ½ oz. each) red kidney beans, partially drained

Cook and stir onions and bell pepper in oil. Add beef; cook until browned. Drain fat. Stir in chili powder, then add tomatoes, tomato sauce, ketchup, salt and pepper. Simmer, uncovered, 30 minutes, stirring occasionally. Add beans; simmer 15 minutes. Makes 8 servings.

USING HEINZ TOMATO KETCHUP IN U.S.

CHARLES REICHBLUM'S BAKED BEANS

1 small onion chopped
1 large can (16 oz.) Heinz Vegetarian Beans
1/3 cup Heinz Hot Ketchup
3 tablespoons brown sugar

In a baking dish mix chopped onions, Heinz
Vegetarian Beans, Hot Ketchup, and brown sugar.
Cover and bake in 400°F for 25 minutes, until
mixture is bubbling around the edges. Makes 3
servings.

JOHN DRYER'S FAVORITE BAKED BEANS

1 can (16oz.) Heinz Pork & Beans
1 can (15 oz.) can red kidney beans, drained
1/4 cup Heinz Ketchup
2 tablespoons dark brown sugar
1 tablespoon cooked bacon bits
2 teaspoons dried minced onion
2 teaspoons Heinz Mustard

Combine all ingredients in a 1-1/2 quart casserole.
Bake, uncovered, in a 350°F oven about 45 minutes.

USING HEINZ TOMATO KETCHUP IN U.S.

HEINZ "TK" TACOZ

1 lb. ground turkey or beef
1 pkg. (1-1/4 oz.) taco seasoning mix
1/2 cup water
1/2 cup Heinz Tomato Ketchup
10 taco shells
Shredded lettuce
Chopped tomatoes
Shredded Cheddar cheese
Sour Cream

Cook turkey or beef until no longer pink. Stir in taco seasoning mix and water. Simmer 2 minutes or until slightly thickened. Stir in ketchup; heat. Spoon meat mixture into taco shells. Top with lettuce, tomatoes, cheese and sour cream as desired. Makes 5 servings.

USING HEINZ TOMATO KETCHUP IN U.S.

CRANBERRY ORANGE CHICKEN

4   skinless, boneless chicken breast halves
1   tablespoon vegetable oil
3/4 cup whole berry cranberry sauce
1/2 cup Heinz Tomato Ketchup
3   tablespoons frozen orange juice concentrate
2   tablespoons orange marmalade
1/8 teaspoon cloves

In large skillet, brown chicken in oil; remove and set aside. Add cranberry sauce and remaining ingredients. Heat, stirring, until cranberry sauce is melted. Return chicken to skillet; spoon sauce over. Cover; simmer 10 minutes or until chicken is no longer pink and juices run clear. Makes 4 servings.

USING HEINZ TOMATO KETCHUP IN U.S.

LOVE APPLE PIE

1/3 cup Heinz Tomato Ketchup
2   teaspoons lemon juice
6   cups sliced peeled tart cooking apples (about 2
      pounds)
2/3 cup all-purpose flour
1/3 cup granulated sugar
1 teaspoon cinnamon
1/3 cup butter or margarine, softened
1 unbaked 9-inch pie shell

Blend ketchup and lemon juice (if apples are very
tart, add 1 to 2 teaspoons granulated sugar to ketchup
mixture); combine with apples. For topping,
combine flour, sugar and cinnamon; cut in butter
until thoroughly mixed. Fill pie shell with apples;
sprinkle topping over apples. Bake in 425°F oven, 40
to 45 minutes or until apples are cooked. Serve warm
with ice cream, if desired. Makes one 9-inch pie.

USING HEINZ CHILI SAUCE IN U.S.

CORNED TOP BEEF PIE

1-1/2 pounds lean ground beef
1/2 cup chopped celery
1 bottle (12 oz.) Heinz Chili Sauce
1 unpeeled tart apple, chopped
1/4 teaspoon pepper
1/4 teaspoon cumin
1 package (6.3 to 9 oz.) corn muffin mix
1 can (7 to 8-3/4 oz.) whole kernel corn, drained

Brown beef and celery in large skillet; drain. Stir in
chili sauce, apple, pepper and cumin. Spoon meat
mixture into a 10-inch quiche dish or an 8- or 9-inch
square baking pan. Prepare corn muffin mix
following package directions. Stir corn into muffin
batter. Spread batter evenly over meat mixture to
outer edges of dish. Bake in 400°F oven, 30 to 35
minutes or until cornbread is golden brown. Let
stand 5 to 10 minutes before serving. Makes 6
servings.

USING HEINZ CHILI SAUCE IN U.S.

CHILI SALSA

1 bottle (12 oz.) Heinz Chili Sauce
1/2 cup finely chopped green pepper
1/2 cup finely chopped yellow or red bell pepper
1/2 cup finely chopped onion
1 to 2 teaspoons minced fresh cilantro

In medium bowl, combine all ingredients. Serve with grilled chicken, beef or fish or tortilla chips. Store any leftover salsa in refrigerator. Makes about 2 cups.

USING HEINZ 57 SAUCE IN U.S.

PORK CHOPS JALAPEÑO

1/2 cup Heinz 57 Sauce
1/4 cup jalapeño pepper jelly
1 tablespoon lime juice
1 tablespoon lemon juice
1 teaspoon Heinz Worcestershire Sauce
1/2 to 1 teaspoon minced fresh jalapeño pepper
1/4 teaspoon salt
1/4 teaspoon garlic powder
1/8 teaspoon pepper
1-1/2 pounds boneless pork loin, cut into 6 equal
     slices
1 tablespoon vegetable oil

In small bowl, combine 57 Sauce and next 8
ingredients; blend well and set aside. Trim excess fat
from pork. Quickly brown chops in oil on both sides;
drain and discard drippings. Pour reserved 57 Sauce
mixture over chops. Cook, uncovered, 8 to 10
minutes or until pork is cooked. Thicken sauce with
cornstarch-water mixture, if desired. Makes 6
servings.

USING HEINZ 57 SAUCE IN U.S.

ORANGE ALMOND SAUCE

1 jar (12 oz.) sweet orange marmalade
1/4 cup Heinz 57 Sauce
2 tablespoons minced onion
2 teaspoons lemon juice
1 teaspoon soy sauce
1/4 teaspoon ginger
1/8 teaspoon red pepper
1/8 teaspoon allspice
1/4 cup sliced almonds

Combine orange marmalade, 57 Sauce, onion, lemon juice, soy sauce, ginger, red pepper and allspice in small saucepan. Cook over medium-low heat 10 minutes or until hot, stirring occasionally. Stir in almonds. Serve over pork, ham, chicken or duck. Makes about 1-1/2 cups.

USING HEINZ 57 SAUCE AND VINEGAR IN U.S.

SOUTHWEST CAVIAR

3 cans (16 oz. each) black-eyed peas, drained,
  divided
1 tablespoon Heinz Gourmet Wine Vinegar
1/2 cup Heinz 57 Sauce
1 clove garlic, minced
1/2 cup chopped green pepper
1/2 cup chopped red bell pepper
1 cup chopped onions
1 medium tomato, seeded, chopped
1 jalapeño pepper, seeded, chopped
1 tablespoon chopped fresh cilantro
1/2 teaspoon chili powder
1/4 teaspoon salt
1/4 teaspoon cumin

Place 1-1/2 cups peas in food processor or blender.
Add vinegar and 57 Sauce. Cover and process until
smooth. Combine pureed pea mixture, whole peas,
garlic and remaining ingredients; blend well. Chill.
Serve as a dip with corn chips or on lettuce as a salad.
Makes 6 cups.

USING HEINZ VINEGAR IN U.S.

CHICKEN TACOS

1/2 cup Heinz Tomato Ketchup
1 tablespoon Heinz Vinegar
1 jalapeño pepper, seeded, minced
1/4 teaspoon garlic powder
1/4 teaspoon cumin
4 skinless boneless chicken breast halves (about 1
    pound), cut into 1/8-inch strips
1 tablespoon vegetable oil
8 taco shells, heated
Shredded cheese, shredded lettuce, tomato chunks,
    sliced green onions, sliced ripe olives, dairy sour
    cream

Combine first 5 ingredients; set aside. In large skillet,
sauté chicken in oil until lightly browned, about 3 to
4 minutes. Stir in reserved ketchup mixture.
Simmer, uncovered, 15 minutes, stirring
occasionally. Spoon chicken filling into taco shells.
Serve with cheese, lettuce, tomato, onions, olives,
sour cream as desired. Makes 4 servings (about 2
cups chicken mixture).

USING HEINZ VINEGAR IN U.S.

FAMILY FRENCH DRESSING

1/2 cup Heinz Tomato Ketchup
1/2 cup vegetable oil
1/4 cup Heinz Apple Cider Vinegar
1 tablespoon confectioners sugar
1 clove garlic, split
1/4 teaspoon salt
Dash pepper

Combine ingredients in jar; cover and shake
vigorously. Chill to blend flavors. Remove garlic;
shake again before serving over tossed green salads.
Makes 1-1/4 cups.

USING STARKIST TUNA IN U.S.

Cool-served recipes are always in good taste. Try chilling the empty plates (10 minutes in the freezer, 20 minutes in the refrigerator) to keep your food as cool as spring.

GARDEN BOW TIE PASTA

2 (6 oz.) cans StarKist Tuna, drained and chunked
1/2 pound Farfalle (bow tie pasta)
2 tablespoons olive oil
1 cup sliced onions
1/4 pound sliced portabella mushrooms
1 cup white wine
3 tablespoons fresh thyme or 1 tablespoon dried
4 cups frozen vegetable medley
  garlic salt and pepper to taste

Cook pasta according to package directions, drain; rinse. In large skillet, heat olive oil over medium-high heat; sauté onions and mushrooms for 3-5 minutes. Add wine and continue cooking 2 minutes. Add thyme, tuna, vegetables and mix gently. Add pasta; season with garlic salt and pepper; heat 3-4 minutes. Garnish option; grated Parmesan cheese. Serves 6.

USING STARKIST TUNA IN U.S.

CLASSIC TUNA SANDWICH

2 (6 oz.) cans StarKist Tuna, drained and chunked
1/2 cup chopped celery
1/4 cup mayonnaise
2 tablespoons chopped black olives or sweet pickle
   relish—(for Mediterranean twist, use dill pickles
   and capers instead of olives or relish)
1 hard-cooked egg, chopped
2 teaspoons lemon pepper seasoning
2 teaspoons lemon juice
8 slices bread
   curly-leaf lettuce leaves

In medium bowl, combine all ingredients except
bread; mix well. Chill several hours. Line 4 slices of
bread with lettuce, top each with 1/4 tuna mixture,
and top with the remaining bread. Serves 4.

USING STARKIST TUNA IN U.S.

ALBACORE WITH LEMON SAUCE

2 cups pasta shells, uncooked
1 (6-1/8 oz.) can StarKist Solid White Albacore in
   spring water, drained
1 tablespoon butter
1/2 cup chicken broth
1/4 cup dry white wine
2 tablespoons lemon juice
1 tablespoon corn starch
1 teaspoon lemon pepper seasoning, dried basil
   or dillweed
1 tablespoon finely chopped green onion

Cook shells according to package directions. Drain
and place in serving bowl. Mix in Albacore.
In same pot, melt butter. Mix remaining ingredients
together, except green onions, until corn starch is
dissolved and add to pot. Bring sauce to a boil,
stirring constantly. Continue boiling for 1 minute,
stirring occasionally.   Season to taste with salt,
pepper and a pinch of sugar. Pour sauce over
Albacore and shells. Sprinkle with green onion.
Makes 3 servings.

USING HEINZ BIG RED TOMATO SOUP IN AUSTRALIA

'BIG RED' CHOCOLATE CAKE

2-1/4 cups self-raising flour
1/3 cup cocoa
1 teaspoon bicarbonate of soda
1-1/2 teaspoons cinnamon
1 teaspoon ground ginger
1-1/3 cups caster sugar
420g can Heinz Big Red Tomato Soup
2 eggs
125g butter, melted
1/4 cup water

Sift dry ingredients into a large bowl. Add wet ingredients, mix to combine. Using electric beaters, beat on high speed for three minutes. Pour into a greased and lined 23cn round cake pan. Bake in a preheated oven to 180°Celsius (350° F) for 1 to 1-1/4 hours or until a skewer inserted into the centre of the cake comes out clean. Leave in pan for 10 minutes before removing to a wire rack to cool completely. Top with a chocolate frosting and serve garnished with chocolate shavings and strawberries.

USING WATTIE'S BAKED BEANS IN NEW ZEALAND

BAKED BEAN AND BACON MUFFINS

1 small onion, peeled and finely chopped
3 rashers (slices) bacon, diced
3 cups self-rising flour
1/2 teaspoon each salt and pepper
1/4 cup chopped fresh parsley
1-1/2 cups grated tasty cheese
425g can Wattie's Baked Beans
2 eggs
1-1/4 cups milk
1 tablespoon whole grain mustard
100g butter, melted

Cook the onion and bacon in a non -stick frying pan until softened and cooked. Cool. Sift the self-rising flour, salt and pepper into a large bowl. Stir in the parsley and 1 cup of the grated cheese. Make a well in the centre. Mix the onion mixture, Wattie's Baked Beans, eggs, milk and whole grain mustard together and pour into the dry ingredients. Stir gently to mix, adding the melted butter as you stir. Divide the mixture evenly among 12 large well-greased muffin tins and sprinkle the tops with a little of the remaining grated cheese. Bake at 200°C (400°F) for 15-20 minutes until well risen and golden. Cool in the tins 2-3 minutes before transferring to a cake rack. Serve warm. Makes 12 large muffins.

USING HEINZ TOMATO KETCHUP, TOMATO JUICE, MUSTARD AND WORCESTERSHIRE IN CANADA

SHEPHERD'S PIE

500 g (1 pound) lean ground beef
1 medium onion, chopped
15ml (1 tablespoon) vegetable oil
1x300g frozen mixed vegetables
125 ml (1/2 cup) Heinz Tomato Ketchup
50 ml (1/4 cup) Heinz Tomato Juice
15 ml (1 tablespoon) Heinz Mustard
5 ml (1 teaspoon) Heinz Worcestershire Sauce
5 ml (1 teaspoon) each; salt and pepper
4 servings prepared mashed potatoes

Cook and stir beef and onion in hot oil until beef is no longer pink. Add remaining ingredients except the prepared potatoes. Bring mixture to a boil and simmer uncovered for 15 minutes, stirring occasionally. Spoon into a 2L (2 quart) casserole dish. Top with prepared potatoes. Bake at 180°C (350°F) for about 15 to 20 minutes or until potatoes are lightly browned. Serves 4 to 6.

USING HEINZ CHILI SAUCE IN CANADA

POTTED CHEESE SPREAD

500 ml (16 oz.) grated Old Cheddar
125g (1 package) cream cheese, softened
50 ml (1/4 cup) Heinz Chili Sauce
25 ml (2 tablespoons) dry sherry
2 ml (1/2 teaspoon) dry mustard

Blend all ingredients until smooth. Pack into a crock or serving dish. Chill several hours. (May be stored in refrigerator up to a week.) Serve with crackers or apple slices. Makes 450 ml (1-3/4 cups).

USING HEINZ CEREAL or PABLUM IN CANADA

SUNNY DAY COOKIES

150 ml (2/3 cup) butter or margarine
250 ml (1 cup) lightly packed brown sugar
1 egg
5 ml (1 teaspoon) vanilla
175 ml (3/4 cup) sifted all-purpose flour
2 ml (1/2 teaspoon) baking soda
500 ml (2 cups) Heinz Cereal or Pablum (any
    variety)

Cream butter and sugar. Beat in egg and vanilla.
Mix together flour, soda and Heinz cereal. Blend
into creamed mixture. Shape into small balls or drop
by spoonfuls onto lightly greased baking sheet.
Flatten with floured fork. Bake in 190°C (375°F)
oven for 10-12 minutes. Makes about 3 dozen.

USING HEINZ CHILI SAUCE, WORCESTERSHIRE SAUCE AND MUSTARD IN CANADA

COUNTRY STYLE RIBS

1 kg (2 pounds) pork ribs, cut into serving-size pieces
285 ml (1 bottle) Heinz Chili Sauce
1 clove garlic, minced
25 ml (2 tablespoons) chopped onion
25 ml (2 tablespoons) lemon juice
15 ml (1 tablespoon) Heinz Worcestershire Sauce
15 ml (1 tablespoon)Heinz Prepared Mustard
15 ml (1 tablespoon) brown sugar
1 ml (1/4 teaspoon) salt

Place ribs in a 3.5L (9" x 13") baking dish. Mix together remaining ingredients. Pour sauce mixture over ribs; cover with foil. (Dish can be prepared ahead to this point and refrigerated.) Bake covered in 180°C (350°F) oven for 1 hour or until tender, basting occasionally with sauce. To brown (optional): barbecue or broil, brushing with extra sauce about 5 minutes each side. Serves 4.

USING HEINZ TOMATO KETCHUP IN THE U.K.

RED EYES

1 tablespoon oil
1 small onion, finely chopped
1 garlic clove, crushed
3 tomatoes, peeled, thinly sliced
salt and black pepper
1/4 teaspoon dried basil
1/4 teaspoon paprika
25g Heinz Tomato Ketchup
2 slices hot buttered toast
2 eggs, poached

Heat oil, add onions and garlic and fry until onion is
soft. Add tomatoes, salt, pepper, basil, paprika and
Heinz Tomato Ketchup; mix well and continue
cooking for about 5 minutes to blend the flavours.
Spoon the mixture on to slices of toast, and put
poached eggs on top. Serve at once. Serves 1.

USING HEINZ TOMATO KETCHUP IN THE U.K.

RED ROOSTER OMELETTE

6 eggs
6 teaspoons water
salt and pepper
25g butter
1 teaspoon mixed herbs
50g Heinz Tomato Ketchup
100g ham, chopped
2 tomatoes, skinned and sliced
50g Mozzarella or Edam cheese

Beat eggs with water, salt and pepper. Melt butter in omelette pan. Turn up the heat. Pour in egg mixture and draw the mixture to the middle of the pan with a fork. Once the mix is almost set, sprinkle on the herbs. Mix Heinz Tomato Ketchup and ham together, spread over omelette. Arrange slices of tomato on top. Cover with cheese slices and place under hot grill until the cheese melts. Serve at once. Serves 2.

Addresses for free gifts from Heinz

57th Wedding Anniversary:
> Send a copy of your marriage certificate and a letter signed by the wife and husband to:

> > Happy 57th Anniversary
> > H.J. Heinz Co.
> > P.O. Box 57
> > Pittsburgh, PA 15230-0057 USA

Pickle and Ketchup Pins:
> For free pickle and ketchup pins, write to:

> > Heinz Pickle and Ketchup Pins
> > P.O. Box 57
> > Pittsburgh, PA   15230 USA

Heinz Hitch Appearances

Those wanting to have the Hitch at a future event should write to Jack Horner Communications, Inc., 902 Brinton Road, Pittsburgh, PA 15221 USA or call 1-412-473-3400. The Heinz Hitch schedules appearances six to twelve months in advance.

So for an easy address to remember for all other inquiries on products:

Heinz, to honor their slogan, "57 Varieties," has Post Office Box 57 for their World Headquarters in Pittsburgh, Pennsylvania.

Their complete address is:

H.J. Heinz Co.
P.O. Box 57
Pittsburgh, PA 15230-0057. USA.

Their phone number also has a 57...
412-456-5700.

Other books in the
Knowledge in a Nutshell™
series:

Knowledge in a Nutshell…astound your family and stump your friends with…the man who was present when THREE U.S. Presidents were assassinated…the U.S. state that no longer exists…what were the biggest animals that ever lived (it wasn't the dinosaurs)…who was the youngest U.S. President (it wasn't John Kennedy).

Knowledge in a Nutshell on Sports…over 500 amazing fun facts…a treasure chest for sports trivia buffs…find out about the batter who caught his own home run…the great team that never existed…why golf courses have 18 holes…the six-inch home run.

Knowledge in a Nutshell™ products available:

Knowledge in a Nutshell - **The Edible Game-**
a smart cookie

Knowledge in a Nutshell - **Sweet Smarts—**
the candy with a brain

Call 1-800-NUTSHELL (U.S./Canada only)
All others call 1-412-765-2020 or visit our Web site
www.knowledgeinanutshell.com

If you have an interesting fact, and the story behind it, for future **Knowledge in a Nutshell™** books, send it along. We will pay $10 for every fact and its story that we use in the book – and we'll acknowledge you as the contributor. Please write us at:

Knowledge in a Nutshell, Inc.
1420 Centre Ave. Suite 2216
Pittsburgh, PA 15219 USA.

For bulk sales or other questions

Call 1-800-NUTSHELL (U.S./Canada only)
All others call 1-412-765-2020 or visit our Web site
www.knowledgeinanutshell.com

NOTE:. Quantity discounts are available.

QUOTES FROM RADIO TALK SHOW HOSTS ON *KNOWLEDGE IN A NUTSHELL*

"*Knowledge in a Nutshell* is the king of trivia books."
Dave Perkul, WAAM, Ann Arbor, Mich.

"This is the quintessential bathroom book."
Charles Brennen, KMOX, St. Louis, Mo.

" This book belongs in every home. You can amaze
your friends with it."
Bob Christopher, WWL, New Orleans, La.

"Of all the trivia books we have—and we collect
them—this is the best I've seen. These are not just
facts, but wonderful stories."
Phil Gibson and Robb Hough, KLFJ,
Springfield, Mo.

"This book is fun. You got to get this book."
John Cigna, KDKA, Pittsburgh, Pa.

QUOTES FROM RADIO TALK SHOW HOSTS ON *KNOWLEDGE IN A NUTSHELL ON SPORTS*

"*Knowledge in a Nutshell on Sports* is a great sports book to have."
>Andy Furman, WWL, Cincinnati, Ohio

"This is a fabulous book. We think we know a lot about sports, but this book has great stuff we never knew. Wonderful stories."
>Angelo Cataldi and Al Morganti, WIP, Philadelphia, Pa.

"*Knowledge in a Nutshell on Sports* is not just for American sports fans. It's as much fun for us Canadians."
>Paul McDonald, CKLW, Windsor, Ont. Can.

"You think you know sports, but the stories in this book really raise your eyebrows."
>Mike Schopp, WHTK, Rochester, N.Y.